MASTERING RETIREMENT

20 Proven Strategies for Lasting Wealth Happiness and Fulfillment

James A Smith

Table of Contents

INTRODUCTION 4

REDEFINING RETIREMENT 6

THE PILLARS OF WEALTH IN RETIREMENT 12

SMART INVESTING 20

THE POWER OF HEALTH IN RETIREMENT 28

SOCIAL FULFILLMENT 36

PURSUING LIFELONG LEARNING AND PERSONAL GROWTH 44

CREATING PURPOSE 52

LEGACY PLANNING 61

EXPLORING THE WORLD IN RETIREMENT 68

THE EMOTIONAL SIDE OF RETIREMENT 75

MASTERING TIME 81

THE GOLDEN YEARS 89

PROTECTING YOUR WEALTH 94

DOWNSIZING AND SIMPLIFYING 100

20 PROVEN STRATEGIES FOR LASTING WEALTH, HAPPINESS, AND FULFILLMENT 106

CONCLUSION 115

REFERENCES 117

ABOUT THE AUTHOR 120

DISCLAIMER 122

COPYRIGHT 123

LEGAL NOTICE 124

Introduction

In today's fast-paced world, retirement isn't just an end; it's a new beginning. "Mastering Retirement: 20 Proven Strategies for Lasting Wealth, Happiness, and Fulfillment" is a comprehensive guide to crafting a fulfilling retirement lifestyle while securing financial freedom and personal satisfaction. Authored by James Smith, this book combines decades of research, expert advice, and real-world experiences to provide readers with a blueprint for achieving a successful retirement.

Retirement means different things to different people. For some, it's a chance to pursue long-held dreams, from travel adventures to dedicating time to hobbies, volunteering, or spending time with family. For others, it's an opportunity to build new income streams, grow wealth strategically, and secure a legacy. No matter your vision, "Mastering Retirement" offers actionable strategies tailored to meet individual goals, providing a roadmap that aligns with your financial and emotional needs.

This book addresses the critical areas essential for a fulfilling retirement: financial planning, lifestyle design, health and wellness, and the pursuit of purpose and joy. Smith presents a step-by-step approach to financial stability, exploring methods for sustaining and even expanding your wealth, protecting assets, and adapting to unforeseen financial challenges. From investments and passive income to tax strategies and estate planning, each chapter delivers insights designed to bolster financial resilience.

But financial security is only part of the equation. "Mastering Retirement" emphasizes holistic well-being, offering strategies to maintain physical health, nurture mental acuity, and build meaningful connections. Smith delves into the psychological shifts that come with retirement, providing tools to tackle challenges like identity shifts, finding new social circles, and staying mentally sharp. Additionally, readers will find guidance on how to create a legacy that not only reflects their achievements but also passes on values and lessons to future generations.

Through practical advice, expert insights, and inspirational stories from retirees who have successfully transitioned to this new phase, James Smith provides a clear and empowering pathway to a retirement filled with purpose, prosperity, and happiness. Whether you're on the cusp of retirement or planning years in advance, "Mastering Retirement" equips you with the knowledge and confidence to transform this new stage into the most rewarding chapter of your life.

REDEFINING RETIREMENT

Retirement has long been seen as the ultimate goal of the working years—a time when the pressures of earning a living can finally be set aside. The common narrative emphasizes financial independence: save, invest wisely, and ensure your savings outlast your years. While financial security is a critical foundation, viewing retirement solely through the lens of wealth accumulation is limiting.

In today's world, retirement is evolving into something much more dynamic. It's not just about leaving behind the daily grind; it's about embarking on a new chapter of life filled with opportunities for personal growth, meaning, and fulfillment. This shift calls for a reevaluation of what retirement truly means and how to prepare for it beyond dollars and cents.

The Financial Trap: Why Money Isn't Enough

For decades, the message has been clear: retirement is about amassing a large enough nest egg to ensure that you never have to worry about running out of money. This focus on financial independence often means sacrificing personal time, family, and experiences during one's working years to stockpile wealth. The problem with this approach is that it overlooks the other aspects of life that contribute to true fulfillment.

Consider the stories of many who retire with millions of dollars, only to find themselves lost, bored, and disillusioned. The lack of a clear purpose post-retirement can lead to depression, anxiety, or even a premature decline in physical and mental health. While money can certainly buy comfort and security, it cannot provide meaning, connection, or a sense of contribution. This realization leads us to an important question: If not just money, then what should retirement be about?

The New Meaning of Retirement

Retirement is no longer a time to merely rest on one's laurels. The modern retiree has the ability and freedom to reimagine life's possibilities. With increased life expectancy and better health in later years, many retirees now find themselves with decades of time ahead of them. Rather than fading into the background, this period can be a launchpad for new endeavors.

The key is to see retirement not as the end, but as a new beginning—a period in life that offers an opportunity for self-reinvention. The earlier you prepare mentally for this transformation, the more you will be able to take full advantage of your post-work years.

In this new paradigm, retirement becomes about reconnecting with passions that may have been sidelined during the working years. It's about learning new skills, exploring creative pursuits, deepening relationships, and even embarking on new career paths if one so desires. Instead of focusing solely on what you are retiring from (your job), the focus shifts to what you are retiring to—an entirely new way of living.

Reinvention: The Power of Second (or Third) Acts

One of the most exciting aspects of modern retirement is the ability to completely reinvent yourself. Retirement can be a period of personal exploration—an opportunity to try things you didn't have time for earlier in life. Many retirees are going back to school, starting businesses, or learning skills they never had the time to pursue before.

Take, for instance, the growing number of retirees who are embarking on "encore careers"—jobs or volunteer opportunities that align more closely with their values and passions. These careers might pay less than previous roles, but they offer a deep sense of satisfaction because they allow retirees to contribute meaningfully to society. Whether it's teaching, mentoring, or working for a nonprofit, these second acts can bring a sense of purpose and fulfillment that is often missing in traditional retirement.

But reinvention doesn't have to mean jumping into a new job or career. It could also be about rekindling old passions or hobbies that you had to set aside during your working years. Perhaps you once loved painting or playing a musical instrument, but the demands of work and family pushed those pursuits to the back burner. Retirement gives you the freedom to dive back into those activities without the constraints of time or obligation.

The beauty of reinvention in retirement is that it's entirely up to you. There are no rules, no societal expectations to meet. You get to design this phase of your life in whatever way brings you the most joy and fulfillment.

Finding Meaning and Purpose in Retirement

One of the biggest challenges retirees face is finding a sense of purpose. For many, work was not only a source of income but also a source of identity. Without the structure and routine of a job, retirees can feel aimless or adrift. This is why it's crucial to have a plan for how you'll spend your time and energy during retirement, beyond simply managing your finances.

Purpose doesn't have to come from paid work; it can come from a variety of sources. Volunteering, mentoring, or taking part in community organizations can provide a deep sense of fulfillment. Being able to contribute to something larger than yourself, even in small ways, can help you maintain a sense of purpose and meaning in retirement.

For some, spirituality or religion may become a greater focus during this phase of life. Retirement offers the time and space to explore deeper questions of existence and to connect more fully with a higher purpose. Whether through meditation, religious practice, or philosophical study, engaging with spiritual pursuits can add depth and meaning to your retirement years.

Embracing Lifelong Learning

Another key aspect of redefining retirement is embracing the idea of lifelong learning. Far from being the end of your intellectual journey, retirement can be the perfect time to learn new things, expand your mind, and challenge yourself in new ways.

Many retirees find great joy in pursuing education later in life, whether it's through formal courses, self-study, or simply reading more deeply into subjects of interest. With online platforms like Coursera, edX, and YouTube, you can learn almost anything from the comfort of your home. Some retirees choose to go back to college and earn degrees, while others focus on hobbies like photography, cooking, or even learning new languages.

Lifelong learning not only keeps your mind sharp, but it also enriches your life by exposing you to new ideas, perspectives, and cultures. It helps you stay curious, engaged, and open to new experiences—all of which are essential for a fulfilling retirement.

Building Meaningful Relationships

While the financial aspect of retirement is often front and center in discussions, the importance of maintaining and building relationships cannot be overstated. The loss of work-related social interactions can sometimes leave retirees feeling isolated or disconnected. That's why it's essential to invest in relationships with family, friends, and new communities.

Retirement offers the chance to deepen existing relationships by spending more time with loved ones. It's also an opportunity to build new connections through clubs, volunteer organizations, or social groups. Having a strong social network is one of the most important predictors of a happy, healthy retirement. Studies have shown that retirees with rich social lives tend to live longer, healthier lives, and experience greater overall satisfaction.

It's important to be proactive about building and maintaining these relationships. While work may have provided a built-in social circle, retirement requires a more intentional effort to stay connected and engaged with others. Whether through regular meetups with friends, joining a book club, or participating in community activities, staying socially active is key to finding fulfillment in retirement.

The Emotional Side of Retirement

It's also important to recognize that retirement brings significant emotional changes. Leaving behind the structure, routine, and identity that a career provides can trigger feelings of loss or confusion. These emotions are completely normal, but they are often overlooked in traditional discussions about retirement.

As you transition into retirement, it's crucial to acknowledge and address these emotional shifts. Taking time to reflect on what gives your life meaning, and what you want this next phase to look like, can help ease the emotional challenges. Therapy or counseling may also be helpful during this time, especially if you find yourself struggling to adjust.

THE PILLARS OF WEALTH IN RETIREMENT

Retirement is often described as the golden years—a time to relax, enjoy life, and pursue passions without the constant pressure of earning a living. However, achieving this ideal state hinges on one key element: financial freedom. Without a secure financial foundation, the dream of a carefree retirement can quickly turn into a source of anxiety and stress. But financial freedom in retirement goes beyond simply accumulating savings; it's about mastering strategies that allow your wealth to grow, provide a steady income, and last for the entirety of your retirement.

In this chapter, we will explore the pillars of wealth that are essential to securing financial stability in retirement. We will look at various income streams, investment strategies, and financial practices that ensure your wealth not only sustains you but continues to grow throughout your retirement years.

The Foundation: Planning for Longevity

The first pillar of wealth in retirement is planning for the long haul. Many people underestimate how long they will live in retirement, and this miscalculation can lead to financial shortfalls later in life. With advancements in healthcare and an increased focus on healthy living, it's not uncommon for retirees to live 20, 30, or even more years beyond their working life.

Planning for longevity means taking a conservative approach to how much you withdraw from your savings each year and making sure your investment strategy accounts for inflation, market fluctuations, and potential health-related expenses. You want to ensure that your money lasts as long as you do, and this requires careful foresight.

The rule of thumb for withdrawals has traditionally been the "4% rule," where you withdraw 4% of your retirement savings each year to ensure your money lasts. However, given the unpredictability of markets and the ever-changing financial landscape, many experts now advise adjusting this figure based on your needs and circumstances. This could mean starting with a lower withdrawal rate in the early years of retirement or adjusting your withdrawals based on market performance.

Income Streams: More Than Just Savings

A common misconception about retirement is that once you stop working, you'll be solely dependent on the money you've saved over the years. While savings are important, relying on a single source of income can be risky. The key to financial freedom in retirement is diversifying your income streams so that you aren't entirely dependent on your savings. This approach reduces risk and ensures that if one source of income diminishes, others can still support your financial needs.

1. Social Security

Social Security is often the first source of income retirees tap into, and it can be a critical component of your retirement income plan. However, the timing of when you start claiming Social Security benefits can greatly affect your financial stability. While you can begin collecting benefits as early as age 62, delaying your claim until full retirement age (typically 66 or 67, depending on your birth year) or even later, can increase your monthly benefits significantly. In fact, for each year you delay past full retirement age, your benefits increase by about 8%. This strategy can result in a more substantial monthly income, which can have a huge impact over the course of a long retirement.

2. Pensions

If you are among the fortunate few who still have access to a pension plan, this can be a valuable source of retirement income. Pensions provide a guaranteed income for life, offering peace of mind that you will have a steady cash flow. However, it's important to understand the details of your pension plan, including the options for taking a lump sum or annuity payments and any survivor benefits for your spouse.

3. Investment Income

Investments are a crucial element of retirement income. Dividend-paying stocks, bonds, and real estate investments can provide regular income while also allowing your principal to continue growing. The goal here is to develop an investment portfolio that balances risk and return, so you aren't overly exposed to market volatility but can still generate income to supplement your other streams.

Dividend-paying stocks, in particular, can be an excellent source of passive income during retirement. Companies that regularly pay dividends tend to be more established and financially stable, which can offer some protection against market downturns. By reinvesting dividends during the early years of retirement and withdrawing them later on, you can grow your wealth while ensuring you have a reliable income stream.

4. Rental Income

Real estate can be a powerful tool for creating passive income in retirement. Whether through residential or commercial properties, rental income provides a steady cash flow that can help cover living expenses and preserve your retirement savings. Owning real estate has the added benefit of potential appreciation, which can further increase your net worth over time.

However, real estate investing isn't without its challenges. Being a landlord requires time and effort to maintain properties, manage tenants, and handle repairs. Some retirees prefer to hire property management companies to reduce the burden, but this comes with additional costs. Alternatively, some choose to invest in Real Estate Investment Trusts (REITs), which allow you to invest in real estate without the hassle of property management, while still earning a share of the profits.

5. Annuities

Annuities are financial products that can provide guaranteed income for life or for a set period, making them a popular choice for retirees seeking stability. With an annuity, you exchange a lump sum of money upfront for a series of payments over time. The key benefit of annuities is the certainty they provide; no matter what happens with the stock market or your other investments, you can rely on a fixed income.

There are several types of annuities, including fixed, variable, and indexed. Each comes with its own set of benefits and risks, so it's essential to understand how they work before purchasing one. Fixed annuities offer a guaranteed payout, but the payments may not keep up with inflation. Variable annuities allow for more growth potential but come with higher risks, while indexed annuities provide a balance between security and growth potential by linking payouts to a market index like the S&P 500.

Managing Debt in Retirement

Debt can be a major obstacle to financial freedom, especially in retirement when your income may be more limited. Ideally, you want to enter retirement with as little debt as possible. High-interest debt, such as credit cards or personal loans, can eat away at your retirement income and create unnecessary stress.

If you are carrying debt into retirement, it's crucial to develop a strategy for paying it down while still maintaining your other financial goals. Prioritize paying off high-interest debt first, as this will free up more of your income to invest or save. Mortgage debt, on the other hand, can be more manageable, especially if you have a low-interest rate. In some cases, it may make sense to continue paying off your mortgage over time rather than using your savings to pay it off in full.

It's also important to avoid accumulating new debt in retirement. Living within your means and sticking to a budget can help ensure that your retirement savings last and that you aren't burdened by financial obligations later in life.

Protecting Against Inflation

Inflation is a silent but powerful force that can erode your purchasing power over time. Even if you have a solid retirement plan, inflation can cause the cost of living to rise, making it more expensive to cover basic needs like housing, healthcare, and food. This is why it's essential to account for inflation in your retirement planning.

One way to protect against inflation is by including assets in your portfolio that tend to perform well during inflationary periods, such as real estate, commodities, and inflation-protected securities like Treasury Inflation-Protected Securities (TIPS). Dividend-paying stocks can also provide some protection, as companies can raise their dividends to keep pace with inflation.

Additionally, it's important to review your budget regularly and adjust your spending as needed. Being mindful of rising costs and making small changes to your lifestyle can help mitigate the impact of inflation and ensure that your retirement savings last.

Healthcare: A Critical Financial Consideration

One of the most significant expenses in retirement is healthcare. As you age, medical costs tend to rise, and long-term care can be especially expensive. Without proper planning, healthcare costs can quickly deplete your retirement savings.

Medicare is a valuable resource for retirees, but it doesn't cover everything. Supplemental insurance, such as Medigap or Medicare Advantage plans, can help fill in the gaps and reduce out-of-pocket expenses. It's also important to factor in the potential costs of long-term care, whether through a long-term care insurance policy or by setting aside savings specifically for this purpose.

Another option is to establish a Health Savings Account (HSA) while you're still working. HSAs offer triple tax advantages—contributions are tax-deductible, the money grows tax-free, and withdrawals for qualified medical expenses are tax-free. Building up an HSA during your working years can provide a valuable resource for covering healthcare costs in retirement.

Estate Planning: Securing Your Legacy

Financial freedom in retirement isn't just about ensuring that you have enough money to live comfortably; it's also about securing your legacy and making sure that your loved ones are taken care of after you're gone. Estate planning is a critical component of financial planning, and it's essential to have a will, trust, or other legal arrangements in place to manage your assets.

An estate plan not only ensures that your wealth is distributed according to your wishes, but it can also minimize the tax burden on your heirs. It's important to work with an attorney or financial planner to create an estate plan that addresses your unique needs and goals.

Achieving financial freedom in retirement requires careful planning, diversification, and a long-term perspective. By building multiple income streams, managing debt, protecting against inflation, and planning for healthcare costs, you can ensure that your retirement years are not only comfortable but truly fulfilling.

Financial freedom is the foundation upon which the rest of your retirement can flourish. With a solid plan in place, you can enjoy the peace of mind that comes with knowing your wealth will last and that you can pursue your passions without financial worry.

SMART INVESTING

One of the most critical aspects of achieving long-term financial freedom in retirement is building an investment portfolio that can stand the test of time. The goal is not only to accumulate wealth leading up to retirement but also to ensure that your investments continue to generate income throughout your retirement years. Smart investing requires careful planning, diversification, and a strategy that can weather the inevitable ups and downs of the financial markets.

Let's go into the key principles of building a resilient retirement portfolio, discuss the importance of asset allocation, and examine strategies for mitigating risk while maximizing returns. Whether you're nearing retirement or already retired, smart investing is crucial to making sure your nest egg grows and sustains you for the long haul.

The Foundation: Setting Clear Financial Goals

Before diving into the mechanics of investing, it's essential to establish clear financial goals. Without a roadmap, it's easy to get lost in the complexity of the investment world. Your investment strategy should be driven by your unique financial objectives, timeline, and risk tolerance.

1. Define Your Retirement Lifestyle

What kind of lifestyle do you want in retirement? Are you planning to travel extensively, downsize to a smaller home, or perhaps spend more time with family? Understanding your lifestyle aspirations will help you determine how much money you need to sustain yourself. For example, a frugal retiree who plans to stay close to home may require a different investment strategy than someone who intends to travel the world or live in a high-cost city. Defining these goals helps you estimate your future expenses and tailor your investments to meet those needs.

2. Establish Your Time Horizon

The next step is understanding your time horizon. The length of time you expect to remain invested impacts your strategy significantly. If you have 20 or more years before you retire, you can afford to take on more risk in your portfolio, as you have time to recover from market downturns. However, if you're already retired or within five years of retirement, you'll need a more conservative approach to protect your wealth. Your time horizon will also help guide your asset allocation, which we'll explore later in the chapter.

3. Assess Your Risk Tolerance

Every investor has a different level of comfort with risk. Some are willing to take bold risks in pursuit of higher returns, while others prefer a more cautious approach. Your risk tolerance will influence how much of your portfolio you allocate to riskier assets, such as stocks, versus safer assets like bonds. It's essential to strike a balance between seeking growth and protecting your capital, especially in retirement when you may have fewer opportunities to recover from market downturns.

Asset Allocation: The Key to a Resilient Portfolio

The backbone of any smart retirement portfolio is asset allocation—how you divide your investments among different asset classes such as stocks, bonds, and cash. Proper asset allocation is crucial for managing risk and ensuring your portfolio is well-positioned for long-term growth.

1. The Importance of Diversification

Diversification is the practice of spreading your investments across various asset classes to reduce risk. The idea is that different types of assets—such as stocks, bonds, and real estate—tend to perform differently under different market conditions. When one asset class underperforms, another may do well, thereby smoothing out your overall returns. This helps protect your portfolio from significant losses in any one area and provides more consistent returns over time.

Diversification also applies within asset classes. For example, instead of investing all your money in U.S. stocks, you might diversify by investing in international stocks, small-cap companies, and different industries. This broader exposure helps mitigate the risk of a downturn in a particular market or sector.

2. The Role of Stocks

Stocks represent ownership in a company and offer the potential for high returns, making them a key component of a retirement portfolio. However, they also come with higher risk, as stock prices can fluctuate significantly. For retirees, the goal is to strike a balance between maintaining exposure to the stock market for growth and reducing the risk of losing capital in a downturn.

A general rule of thumb is to allocate a percentage of your portfolio to stocks based on your age. For instance, the "100 minus your age" rule suggests that if you're 60 years old, you should have 40% of your portfolio in stocks. However, this is just a starting point, and your personal situation—such as your risk tolerance, financial goals, and income needs—should inform your specific allocation.

Within the stock portion of your portfolio, consider investing in a mix of large-cap, mid-cap, and small-cap stocks, as well as international stocks. Large-cap stocks, such as those in the S&P 500, tend to be more stable and offer steady growth, while small-cap stocks can provide higher growth potential but with greater volatility. International stocks give you exposure to markets outside the U.S., which can add another layer of diversification.

3. The Role of Bonds

Bonds are debt securities issued by corporations or governments, and they provide fixed interest payments over time. Bonds are generally considered safer than stocks because they offer more predictable returns. However, the trade-off is that bonds typically provide lower returns than stocks.

For retirees, bonds play a crucial role in providing income and reducing portfolio volatility. Bonds offer a more stable source of income through interest payments, which can help cover living expenses in retirement. In addition, because bonds tend to move inversely to stocks—meaning that when stocks fall, bonds often rise—they can act as a stabilizing force in your portfolio during market downturns.

Consider allocating a portion of your portfolio to a mix of government bonds, corporate bonds, and municipal bonds. Government bonds, such as U.S. Treasury bonds, are considered one of the safest investments, while corporate bonds offer higher returns but with slightly more risk. Municipal bonds, which are issued by local governments, offer tax advantages, as their interest payments are often exempt from federal and sometimes state taxes.

4. Cash and Cash Equivalents

While cash may not offer the same growth potential as stocks or bonds, it provides liquidity and security. Having a portion of your portfolio in cash or cash equivalents, such as money market funds or certificates of deposit (CDs), ensures that you have quick access to money when you need it without having to sell off other investments.

Cash is especially important in retirement to cover short-term expenses and to act as a buffer during market downturns. By keeping enough cash on hand to cover one to two years of living expenses, you can avoid selling your stocks or bonds at a loss if the market is down.

Mitigating Risk: Strategies for Protecting Your Portfolio

Investing always carries risk, but there are several strategies you can use to protect your portfolio, especially as you enter retirement and have less time to recover from losses.

1. Rebalancing Your Portfolio

Over time, the performance of your investments will cause your portfolio's asset allocation to shift. For example, if stocks perform well, they may end up making up a larger portion of your portfolio than you initially intended. This can expose you to more risk than you're comfortable with.

Rebalancing involves periodically adjusting your portfolio to bring it back in line with your target asset allocation. For example, if your allocation to stocks has grown too large, you might sell some of your stock holdings and move the money into bonds or cash. Rebalancing helps you maintain the right balance of risk and reward as you move through different stages of retirement.

2. Dollar-Cost Averaging

Dollar-cost averaging is an investment strategy that involves regularly investing a fixed amount of money, regardless of market conditions. This approach allows you to buy more shares when prices are low and fewer shares when prices are high, effectively averaging out the cost of your investments over time.

For retirees, dollar-cost averaging can be particularly helpful if you're still contributing to an investment account, such as an Individual Retirement Account (IRA) or 401(k). It's a disciplined approach that reduces the emotional impact of market fluctuations and helps you avoid the temptation to time the market—a strategy that rarely works in the long term.

3. Annuities for Guaranteed Income

Annuities are financial products that can provide a guaranteed income stream in retirement. By purchasing an annuity, you trade a lump sum of money for regular payments over a specified period or for the rest of your life. This can be an attractive option for retirees who want to reduce their reliance on market performance for income.

There are different types of annuities, including fixed, variable, and indexed. Each has its pros and cons, so it's essential to understand the details before committing. Fixed annuities provide a guaranteed payout but may not keep up with inflation. Variable annuities allow your payments to grow based on the performance of underlying investments but come with higher risk. Indexed annuities offer a middle ground by linking payments to a market index, such as the S&P 500, while still providing some downside protection.

The Power of Compound Growth

One of the most powerful tools in investing is compound growth, which allows your investments to generate returns on both your initial principal and the returns themselves. Over time, this snowball effect can significantly grow your wealth.

The earlier you start investing, the more time you have to take advantage of compound growth. Even in retirement, compounding can continue to work in your favor if you keep a portion of your portfolio invested in growth assets, such as stocks.

For example, if you invest $100,000 at a 6% annual return, after 20 years, you would have approximately $320,000, thanks to the power of compounding. The key to maximizing compound growth is to stay invested and avoid the temptation to pull money out of your portfolio during market downturns.

The Role of Tax-Efficient Investing

Taxes can have a significant impact on your investment returns, so it's essential to consider tax efficiency when building your retirement portfolio. Strategies like investing in tax-advantaged accounts, such as IRAs and 401(k)s, and using tax-efficient investments, such as index funds, can help minimize the amount you pay in taxes and keep more of your returns working for you.

For retirees, managing withdrawals from tax-deferred accounts and taxable accounts in a tax-efficient manner is crucial. By carefully planning your withdrawals, you can reduce your tax liability and make your money last longer in retirement.

Building a retirement portfolio that lasts requires a careful balance of growth, income, and risk management. By setting clear financial goals, diversifying your investments, and staying disciplined with strategies like rebalancing and dollar-cost averaging, you can create a portfolio that provides long-term financial security. Smart investing isn't about chasing short-term gains; it's about creating a resilient foundation that allows you to enjoy your retirement years with confidence and peace of mind.

THE POWER OF HEALTH IN RETIREMENT

Retirement is often imagined as a time of relaxation, leisure, and fulfillment, but none of this is truly possible without good health. No matter how well you've planned financially, how much you've saved, or how successful your investments have been, your ability to enjoy retirement hinges on your physical and mental well-being. Health is the foundation of everything, and without it, the golden years can quickly become a time of struggle and limitation.

The Connection Between Health and Wealth in Retirement

The relationship between health and wealth is closer than many people realize. Medical expenses are one of the largest and most unpredictable costs in retirement, and poor health can quickly erode even the best-laid financial plans. By prioritizing your health, you can mitigate these risks and maximize your ability to enjoy the fruits of your hard-earned savings.

1. Health as a Financial Asset

Good health is often described as the most valuable form of wealth, especially in retirement. Without it, the financial freedom you've worked so hard to achieve can be overshadowed by medical bills, reduced mobility, and a decreased ability to engage in the activities that bring you joy. On the other hand, maintaining good health allows you to fully experience the pleasures of retirement—whether that's traveling, spending time with family, or pursuing hobbies you love. Moreover, by taking care of your health, you can reduce the burden of healthcare costs, which are often one of the biggest financial concerns for retirees.

Health insurance can help cover some expenses, but it doesn't cover everything. Out-of-pocket costs for medications, procedures, and long-term care can add up quickly. By focusing on preventive health measures—such as regular exercise, a nutritious diet, and routine medical check-ups—you can lower the risk of costly health issues and ensure that your retirement savings last longer.

2. Mental Health and Emotional Well-being

While physical health often takes center stage in discussions about well-being, mental health is just as important, if not more so, in retirement. A lack of purpose, isolation, and the loss of social connections can all lead to mental health issues such as depression and anxiety. Mental health problems, in turn, can lead to physical health issues, creating a vicious cycle that undermines your quality of life.

Staying mentally sharp and emotionally grounded during retirement requires proactive effort. Engaging in mentally stimulating activities, maintaining a strong social network, and finding meaningful pursuits can all contribute to a sense of purpose and mental well-being. Physical exercise, as we will discuss, also plays a crucial role in supporting mental health by releasing endorphins and promoting cognitive function.

The Benefits of Maintaining Physical Fitness in Retirement

Regular physical activity is one of the most powerful tools you have for staying healthy in retirement. Not only does exercise keep your body strong and capable, but it also enhances your mental health, reduces the risk of chronic diseases, and improves your overall quality of life.

1. Longevity and Disease Prevention

One of the most compelling reasons to stay active in retirement is its impact on longevity and disease prevention. Numerous studies have shown that regular exercise can reduce the risk of chronic conditions such as heart disease, diabetes, osteoporosis, and even certain cancers. Exercise helps to regulate blood pressure, improve cholesterol levels, and maintain a healthy weight—all of which are critical factors in preventing illness and prolonging life.

For retirees, exercise doesn't have to be intense to be effective. Even moderate activities like walking, swimming, or cycling can have profound health benefits. The key is consistency. Incorporating regular physical activity into your daily routine can significantly reduce your risk of developing chronic diseases and help you stay healthier for longer.

2. Mobility and Independence

One of the greatest fears many retirees face is the loss of independence. Physical decline can lead to difficulty with everyday tasks, reliance on caregivers, and even the need for assisted living. However, by staying active and maintaining muscle strength, flexibility, and balance, you can preserve your mobility and independence well into old age.

Strength training exercises, in particular, are essential for maintaining muscle mass and bone density, both of which naturally decline as we age. This decline can lead to frailty, falls, and fractures, which are common in older adults. However, regular strength training can slow this process, keeping you stronger and more capable of performing daily activities without assistance. Exercises like weightlifting, resistance band workouts, or even bodyweight exercises such as squats and lunges can all be highly effective in preserving strength and mobility.

Balance and flexibility exercises, such as yoga or tai chi, can also play a significant role in preventing falls, which are a leading cause of injury among retirees. Falls can have devastating consequences, leading to broken bones, lengthy recovery times, and a loss of confidence. By incorporating balance training into your fitness routine, you can improve your stability and reduce your risk of falls.

3. Mental Health and Cognitive Function

The benefits of exercise extend far beyond the physical. Staying active is one of the best things you can do for your mental health and cognitive function in retirement. Regular physical activity has been shown to reduce symptoms of depression and anxiety, boost mood, and improve sleep quality. Exercise triggers the release of endorphins, which are natural mood enhancers, and reduces levels of stress hormones like cortisol.

Exercise also plays a crucial role in maintaining cognitive function as we age. Studies have shown that physical activity can improve memory, attention, and processing speed, and it may even help reduce the risk of developing dementia. Activities that require coordination, balance, and concentration—such as dance, martial arts, or tennis—are particularly effective at keeping the brain sharp.

For retirees, staying mentally engaged is just as important as staying physically active. Combining the two—such as by participating in group fitness classes, taking up new sports or hobbies, or learning a new skill that involves movement—can provide a double benefit, keeping both your body and mind in top shape.

4. Social Connection and Community

One often-overlooked aspect of physical activity in retirement is its role in fostering social connections. Exercise can be a highly social activity, whether it's attending fitness classes, joining a walking group, or participating in sports leagues. These social interactions provide not only physical benefits but also emotional support and a sense of community, which are critical for maintaining mental health and preventing isolation.

Retirement can sometimes be a lonely time, especially if you've left behind a social circle connected to your career. Engaging in group fitness activities is a great way to meet new people, stay connected, and combat loneliness. The friendships you form through these activities can provide a strong support network and enhance your overall sense of well-being.

Nutrition: Fueling a Healthy Retirement

Physical activity is only one part of the equation when it comes to maintaining health in retirement. Proper nutrition is just as important, and it plays a critical role in supporting your physical and mental health. A balanced diet provides the fuel your body needs to function optimally and helps prevent a wide range of health issues.

1. Eating for Longevity

A nutrient-dense diet can significantly impact your longevity and reduce the risk of chronic diseases. In retirement, your nutritional needs may change, but the basic principles of healthy eating remain the same: focus on whole, unprocessed foods rich in vitamins, minerals, and antioxidants.

A diet rich in fruits, vegetables, whole grains, lean proteins, and healthy fats supports heart health, boosts the immune system, and provides the energy you need to stay active. These foods also contain antioxidants and anti-inflammatory compounds that protect against the oxidative stress and inflammation associated with aging.

2. Managing Weight and Metabolism

As you age, your metabolism naturally slows down, which can make it more challenging to maintain a healthy weight. However, maintaining a healthy weight is essential for preventing conditions like heart disease, diabetes, and joint problems, all of which can negatively impact your quality of life in retirement.

Staying physically active and eating a balanced diet are the two most important factors in managing your weight. Prioritizing nutrient-dense foods over empty calories, such as those found in sugary snacks and processed foods, can help you maintain a healthy metabolism and avoid weight gain.

3. Bone and Joint Health

Bone and joint health are especially important in retirement, as age-related bone loss and joint deterioration can lead to conditions like osteoporosis and arthritis. To support bone health, make sure your diet includes adequate amounts of calcium and vitamin D. Dairy products, leafy greens, and fortified foods are excellent sources of calcium, while sunlight and supplements can help you meet your vitamin D needs.

Omega-3 fatty acids, found in fatty fish like salmon, are also important for joint health, as they have anti-inflammatory properties that can help reduce the pain and stiffness associated with arthritis.

4. Hydration and Cognitive Function

Hydration is often overlooked but is critical for maintaining cognitive function and overall health in retirement. Dehydration can lead to confusion, fatigue, and an increased risk of falls. Make sure to drink plenty of water throughout the day, especially if you're engaging in physical activity.

Preventive Care and Regular Check-ups

In addition to staying active and eating well, regular medical check-ups and preventive care are crucial for maintaining your health in retirement. By staying on top of routine screenings and tests, you can catch potential health issues early, when they are more easily treated.

Annual physicals, dental check-ups, and eye exams should all be part of your routine. Depending on your age and health history, your doctor may recommend additional screenings, such as mammograms, colonoscopies, or bone density tests. These preventive measures can help you stay ahead of any potential health problems and ensure that you're in the best possible shape to enjoy your retirement.

Health is the ultimate enabler in retirement. Without it, even the most well-planned financial strategies can feel hollow. By prioritizing physical fitness, mental well-being, and proper nutrition, you can build the foundation for a long, active, and fulfilling retirement. The power of health is a gift that allows you to experience all the joys and opportunities that come with your golden years—so take care of your body, and it will take care of you.

SOCIAL FULFILLMENT

Social fulfillment is a cornerstone of a vibrant and satisfying retirement. While financial security and health are crucial, the quality of your social life can greatly influence your overall happiness and sense of purpose. As we transition into retirement, it becomes essential to nurture existing relationships and build new connections. This chapter delves into the importance of maintaining and enhancing your social networks, providing practical strategies for cultivating meaningful relationships and ensuring you remain engaged with a supportive community.

The Importance of Social Fulfillment in Retirement

Human beings are inherently social creatures, and our well-being is deeply intertwined with our social interactions. In retirement, the shift from a structured work environment to a more self-directed lifestyle can lead to significant changes in social dynamics. For many, this transition can result in feelings of isolation or loneliness if not addressed proactively. Understanding the importance of social fulfillment and actively working to maintain and expand your social connections is key to a rewarding retirement.

1. The Impact of Social Connections on Well-being

Research consistently shows that strong social connections contribute to better mental and physical health. Engaging in meaningful relationships can reduce stress, lower the risk of depression, and even improve longevity. Conversely, social isolation and loneliness are linked to a range of health issues, including increased risk of heart disease, cognitive decline, and weakened immune function.

Social interactions stimulate positive emotions and provide a sense of belonging, which are crucial for mental health. Whether through close family relationships, friendships, or community involvement, having a robust social network can enhance your quality of life and provide a support system during challenging times.

2. Adapting to Changes in Social Dynamics

Retirement often brings significant changes to your social landscape. The loss of daily interactions with colleagues and the transition from a structured work environment can impact your social life. It's important to recognize that while some relationships may naturally shift, others can be maintained or strengthened with deliberate effort.

Additionally, retirement may present opportunities to reconnect with old friends or family members with whom you've lost touch. This period can be a chance to rekindle relationships that have faded due to the demands of work and family life.

Nurturing Existing Relationships

Maintaining strong connections with family and friends requires ongoing effort, especially as life circumstances change. Here are some strategies to ensure you keep these important relationships strong:

1. Regular Communication

In the hustle and bustle of daily life, it's easy for communication with loved ones to become sporadic. Retirement provides more time to nurture these relationships, so make a habit of staying in touch regularly. This can be through phone calls, video chats, or even handwritten letters.

Setting aside specific times each week or month for catching up with family and friends can help ensure that these interactions remain a priority. Even small gestures, like sending a text message or a quick email, can make a significant difference in maintaining closeness.

2. Family Gatherings and Traditions

Family gatherings and traditions can provide opportunities to connect and create lasting memories. Regular family events, such as holiday celebrations, birthdays, or reunions, can strengthen family bonds and offer a sense of continuity.

If you live far from family members, consider organizing virtual gatherings or planning periodic visits. Keeping traditions alive, whether through in-person events or digital means, helps maintain a sense of connection and belonging.

3. Being Present and Engaged

When spending time with loved ones, focus on being present and engaged. Quality interactions are more meaningful than quantity. Show genuine interest in their lives, listen actively, and participate in activities that foster deeper connections.

Avoid distractions during social interactions, such as checking your phone or multitasking. By being fully present, you demonstrate respect and appreciation for the relationship, which strengthens the bond.

4. Supporting and Being Supported

Relationships are a two-way street. Be proactive in offering support to your loved ones when they need it, and don't hesitate to ask for help when you need it. Mutual support reinforces trust and deepens connections.

Whether it's providing a listening ear, offering practical assistance, or simply being there for someone going through a tough time, your support is invaluable. Likewise, allowing others to support you fosters a sense of reciprocity and strengthens the relationship.

Building New Connections

Retirement offers a unique opportunity to expand your social circle and explore new connections. This can be particularly important if you've moved to a new location or if your previous social network has diminished. Here's how to build new connections and enrich your social life:

1. Exploring Hobbies and Interests

Engaging in hobbies and interests is an excellent way to meet like-minded individuals and build new friendships. Whether it's joining a book club, taking a cooking class, or participating in a gardening group, shared interests can provide a natural foundation for connection.

Look for community centers, adult education programs, or online platforms that offer opportunities to explore your interests and connect with others. Participating in group activities not only helps you develop new skills but also introduces you to people who share your passions.

2. Volunteering and Community Involvement

Volunteering is a powerful way to contribute to your community while building new relationships. Whether it's helping at a local food bank, participating in environmental conservation efforts, or assisting in community events, volunteering offers a sense of purpose and connection.

Being actively involved in community activities also helps you stay engaged and informed about local events, which can lead to new social opportunities. Volunteering often brings together people from diverse backgrounds, fostering connections through shared goals and experiences.

3. Joining Social or Support Groups

Many communities offer social or support groups designed for retirees or individuals with specific interests. These groups can provide valuable social interaction and support as you transition into retirement.

Explore local organizations or online communities that focus on topics of interest to you, such as travel, health and wellness, or cultural activities. Joining these groups can help you find new friends and build a sense of belonging.

4. Attending Events and Activities

Keep an eye out for local events and activities that interest you. This could include lectures, concerts, festivals, or workshops. Attending events not only offers entertainment but also provides opportunities to meet new people and engage in your community.

Be open to attending events on your own if needed. Many people find themselves in similar situations, and you may make new connections simply by being present and approachable.

5. Using Technology to Connect

Technology can play a significant role in maintaining and building connections. Social media platforms, video conferencing, and online forums can help you stay connected with family and friends, especially if you're geographically distant.

Engage with online communities that align with your interests or hobbies. Participate in discussions, share your experiences, and build relationships with people who share similar passions. Online tools can also facilitate virtual gatherings with loved ones, helping bridge any distance.

Overcoming Challenges in Social Connectivity

Building and maintaining relationships can come with its own set of challenges. Understanding these challenges and developing strategies to overcome them can help you stay socially fulfilled in retirement.

1. Addressing Loneliness and Isolation

Loneliness can be a significant issue in retirement, especially if you've moved to a new area or experienced the loss of friends or family members. Combat loneliness by actively seeking out social opportunities and staying engaged in activities that interest you.

Consider reaching out to community organizations, joining social clubs, or participating in volunteer work. Regular social interactions and a proactive approach to building new connections can help alleviate feelings of isolation.

2. Navigating Social Changes

As you transition into retirement, you may encounter changes in your social dynamics, such as the need to form new friendships or adjust to shifts in existing relationships. Approach these changes with an open mind and a willingness to adapt.

It's normal for social connections to evolve over time. Embrace the opportunity to meet new people and form new relationships while maintaining efforts to stay connected with existing friends and family.

3. Balancing Social and Personal Time

Balancing social activities with personal time is essential for maintaining a fulfilling retirement. While social interactions are important, it's also crucial to set aside time for yourself and engage in activities that bring you joy and relaxation.

Create a schedule that allows for a healthy balance between social engagements and personal downtime. This balance helps ensure that you remain energized and content in both your social and personal pursuits.

PURSUING LIFELONG LEARNING AND PERSONAL GROWTH

Retirement offers a unique opportunity to delve into lifelong learning and personal growth, allowing you to explore interests and passions that may have been set aside during your working years. Embracing continuous learning and personal development is crucial not only for intellectual stimulation but also for maintaining a sense of purpose and fulfillment.

The Value of Lifelong Learning

Lifelong learning refers to the ongoing, voluntary, and self-motivated pursuit of knowledge for personal or professional development. It is a fundamental aspect of a fulfilling and engaged retirement, offering numerous benefits that go beyond simply acquiring new skills.

1. Cognitive Benefits

Engaging in lifelong learning helps keep your brain active and sharp. Studies show that continuous intellectual stimulation can enhance cognitive function, improve memory, and reduce the risk of cognitive decline associated with aging. Learning new skills, solving problems, and engaging in mentally challenging activities help to create new neural connections and promote brain health.

Activities such as learning a new language, playing a musical instrument, or studying a new subject can be particularly beneficial for cognitive health. These activities not only provide mental stimulation but also encourage creativity and critical thinking.

2. Emotional and Psychological Well-being

Lifelong learning can also have a profound impact on emotional and psychological well-being. The process of learning and personal growth fosters a sense of accomplishment and boosts self-esteem. Pursuing new interests and hobbies provides a sense of purpose and direction, contributing to overall happiness and satisfaction.

Additionally, engaging in learning activities can reduce feelings of boredom and stagnation that might arise in retirement. Having goals and challenges to work towards keeps you motivated and focused, enhancing your overall sense of fulfillment.

3. Social Benefits

Lifelong learning often involves interacting with others, whether through classes, workshops, or discussion groups. These social interactions provide opportunities to meet new people, form connections, and build friendships. Social engagement is crucial for maintaining a vibrant and active social life, which contributes to overall well-being.

Participating in group learning activities or joining clubs and organizations related to your interests can help you expand your social network and stay connected with others who share similar passions.

Discovering New Hobbies and Interests

Retirement is the perfect time to explore new hobbies and interests that you might not have had time for previously. Finding activities that bring joy and fulfillment requires some exploration and self-discovery. Here are some strategies to help you identify and pursue new hobbies and interests:

1. Reflect on Past Interests

Think about hobbies and activities that you enjoyed in the past but may have set aside due to work or other commitments. Revisiting old interests can be a great way to reconnect with activities that brought you joy and satisfaction.

Reflect on what you enjoyed about these activities and how you might reintroduce them into your life. For example, if you used to enjoy painting or gardening, consider taking a class or joining a local club to rekindle your passion.

2. Explore New Areas

Use retirement as an opportunity to step outside of your comfort zone and explore new areas of interest. This might involve trying out new activities that you've always been curious about but never had the chance to pursue.

Consider attending workshops, taking online courses, or visiting local events related to topics you find intriguing. Whether it's learning to cook, trying out a new sport, or delving into creative writing, exploring new areas can open up exciting possibilities for personal growth.

3. Leverage Technology

Technology provides a wealth of resources for discovering and pursuing new hobbies. Online platforms offer a wide range of courses, tutorials, and virtual communities that can help you learn new skills and connect with others who share your interests.

Websites like Coursera, Udemy, and Khan Academy provide online courses on a variety of subjects, from art and music to technology and science. Additionally, social media platforms and forums can connect you with communities and groups focused on specific hobbies and interests.

4. Set Personal Goals

Setting personal goals can provide structure and motivation as you explore new hobbies and interests. Establish clear, achievable goals for what you want to accomplish and create a plan to work towards them.

For example, if you're interested in learning a new language, set a goal to complete a certain number of lessons each week. If you're taking up a new craft or skill, set milestones for completing projects or mastering techniques. Tracking your progress can help you stay motivated and measure your achievements.

5. Join Clubs and Groups

Joining clubs, groups, or organizations related to your interests is an excellent way to immerse yourself in new activities and meet like-minded individuals. Look for local clubs, community centers, or online groups that focus on the hobbies you're interested in.

Being part of a group provides not only social interaction but also opportunities for collaboration and learning from others. Whether it's a book club, hiking group, or cooking class, participating in group activities can enhance your experience and provide a sense of community.

Strategies for Personal Growth

Personal growth encompasses various aspects of self-improvement, including developing new skills, expanding your knowledge, and enhancing your overall well-being. Here are some strategies to help you achieve personal growth in retirement:

1. Pursue Educational Opportunities

Consider enrolling in formal educational programs or classes that interest you. Many universities and educational institutions offer courses specifically designed for retirees or lifelong learners.

Explore options such as continuing education programs, adult education centers, or local community colleges. Subjects may range from academic disciplines to practical skills, providing a wide array of opportunities for intellectual and personal development.

2. Develop New Skills

Acquiring new skills can be both enjoyable and rewarding. Identify areas where you'd like to improve or learn something new, and seek out opportunities to develop those skills.

For example, if you've always wanted to learn to play a musical instrument, take lessons or join a community band. If you're interested in technology, consider taking a course on digital tools or programming. Developing new skills can boost your confidence and provide a sense of accomplishment.

3. Engage in Creative Expression

Creative expression is an important aspect of personal growth. Engaging in creative activities, such as painting, writing, or crafting, allows you to explore your imagination and express yourself in meaningful ways.

Creativity can be a powerful outlet for self-expression and emotional release. It also provides opportunities for problem-solving and innovation, contributing to overall cognitive and emotional well-being.

4. Practice Mindfulness and Reflection

Mindfulness and self-reflection are essential for personal growth. Incorporate practices such as meditation, journaling, or contemplation into your daily routine to gain insights into your thoughts, feelings, and goals.

Mindfulness helps you stay present and focused, while self-reflection allows you to evaluate your progress, identify areas for improvement, and set new objectives. These practices contribute to greater self-awareness and personal development.

5. Embrace Change and Adaptability

Personal growth often involves embracing change and adapting to new circumstances. Be open to new experiences and challenges, and view them as opportunities for growth and learning.

Life in retirement can bring unexpected changes and opportunities. Embracing these changes with a positive attitude and a willingness to adapt can enhance your personal development and overall satisfaction.

The Role of Community and Support Systems

Building a network of support and surrounding yourself with a community that encourages growth and learning is essential for a fulfilling retirement. Seek out connections with individuals who share your interests and values, and engage with organizations that support personal development.

1. Finding a Mentor or Coach

A mentor or coach can provide valuable guidance and support as you pursue new interests and personal growth. Look for individuals who have experience in areas you're interested in and who can offer insights and encouragement.

Mentors can help you set goals, overcome obstacles, and stay motivated. Whether it's a professional mentor, a coach in a specific field, or a trusted friend, having someone to guide and support you can enhance your personal development journey.

2. Participating in Supportive Communities

Joining supportive communities or groups that focus on personal growth can provide additional motivation and encouragement. Look for local or online communities that offer resources, workshops, and events related to your interests.

Being part of a supportive community can provide a sense of belonging and reinforce your commitment to lifelong learning and personal growth. Engage in discussions, share experiences, and contribute to the community to build meaningful connections.

3. Leveraging Online Resources

The internet offers a wealth of resources for personal development and learning. Utilize online platforms, forums, and educational websites to access information, connect with experts, and participate in virtual learning opportunities.

Online resources can provide flexibility and convenience, allowing you to learn and grow at your own pace. Take advantage of webinars, online courses, and virtual workshops to expand your knowledge and skills.

CREATING PURPOSE

Retirement represents a pivotal opportunity to redefine your sense of purpose and contribution. As the structure of your daily life shifts away from professional responsibilities, finding new avenues for meaningful engagement becomes crucial for maintaining a fulfilling and satisfying retirement.

The Importance of Purpose in Retirement

A sense of purpose is essential for a fulfilling retirement. It provides direction, motivation, and a sense of accomplishment, all of which contribute to your overall happiness and satisfaction. Without a clear purpose, you may experience feelings of emptiness or dissatisfaction, which can impact your mental and emotional well-being.

1. Psychological Benefits

Having a sense of purpose contributes to psychological health by providing goals and meaning. It fosters a positive outlook, enhances self-esteem, and reduces the risk of depression and anxiety. When you engage in activities that align with your values and passions, you experience a greater sense of fulfillment and contentment.

Research shows that individuals with a strong sense of purpose are more resilient to stress and adversity. They often have a more optimistic outlook on life and a greater ability to cope with challenges.

2. Physical Health Benefits

A sense of purpose is also linked to better physical health. Studies suggest that individuals who feel they have a purpose are less likely to experience chronic illnesses and have a lower risk of mortality. Engaging in meaningful activities can encourage an active lifestyle, promote better health habits, and contribute to overall longevity.

Purposeful living often involves activities that keep you physically engaged, such as volunteering, exercising, or pursuing hobbies. These activities not only benefit your physical health but also contribute to a greater sense of vitality and well-being.

3. Social and Emotional Well-being

Creating purpose through meaningful activities fosters social connections and emotional fulfillment. Engaging in work or volunteer opportunities provides opportunities to interact with others, build relationships, and contribute to your community.

Meaningful work and contributions can also enhance your emotional well-being by providing a sense of accomplishment and recognition. Feeling valued and appreciated for your contributions reinforces a positive self-image and strengthens your emotional resilience.

Strategies for Finding Meaningful Work

Meaningful work in retirement does not necessarily mean returning to a full-time job; rather, it involves engaging in activities that align with your interests and values. Here are strategies for finding and creating meaningful work that provides a sense of purpose:

1. Exploring Passion Projects

Consider pursuing projects or ventures that align with your passions and interests. This could include starting a small business, launching a creative project, or engaging in a long-held dream or hobby.

Reflect on what activities bring you joy and satisfaction, and explore ways to turn these passions into purposeful endeavors. For example, if you have a passion for writing, consider starting a blog or writing a book. If you enjoy crafting, explore opportunities to sell your creations or teach others.

2. Freelance or Consulting Work

If you miss the professional challenges of your previous career, consider freelance or consulting work in your area of expertise. This allows you to stay engaged in your field while having the flexibility to set your own schedule.

Freelance and consulting opportunities can provide a sense of accomplishment and contribute to your financial well-being. They also offer opportunities to use your skills and experience in a meaningful way, without the demands of a full-time job.

3. Mentoring and Coaching

Sharing your knowledge and experience with others can be a rewarding way to create purpose. Consider becoming a mentor or coach for individuals in your field or community.

Mentoring allows you to provide guidance, support, and encouragement to others, while also offering a sense of fulfillment and legacy. Coaching can involve working with individuals or groups to help them achieve their goals and overcome challenges.

4. Part-Time Employment

If you enjoy the structure and social interaction of work, consider part-time employment in a field that interests you. This allows you to stay engaged professionally while enjoying a more relaxed schedule.

Look for opportunities in areas that align with your values and interests. For example, if you have a passion for education, consider working part-time as a tutor or teaching assistant. If you're interested in the arts, explore opportunities at local galleries or theaters.

Volunteering: Making a Difference in Your Community

Volunteering is a powerful way to create purpose and contribute to your community. It offers numerous benefits, including social engagement, personal satisfaction, and a sense of accomplishment. Here are strategies for finding and engaging in meaningful volunteer opportunities:

1. Identifying Causes and Organizations

Start by identifying causes and organizations that resonate with your values and interests. Reflect on issues that you are passionate about, such as environmental conservation, social justice, animal welfare, or education.

Research local organizations and charities that work in these areas. Many communities have volunteer centers or online platforms that can help you find opportunities that match your interests and skills.

2. Exploring Various Volunteer Roles

Volunteering offers a wide range of roles and responsibilities, from hands-on tasks to administrative support. Consider exploring different types of volunteer work to find roles that align with your skills and interests.

For example, you might volunteer as a mentor for youth programs, assist with fundraising events, provide administrative support for non-profit organizations, or participate in hands-on community service projects.

3. Commitment and Flexibility

Choose volunteer opportunities that fit your schedule and level of commitment. Some roles may require regular weekly involvement, while others offer more flexibility.

It's important to find a balance between your volunteer work and other activities in your life. Look for opportunities that allow you to contribute meaningfully while also providing the flexibility to enjoy other aspects of your retirement.

4. Building Relationships and Networks

Volunteering provides opportunities to meet new people and build relationships within your community. Engage with fellow volunteers and staff members to create a network of connections and support.

Building relationships through volunteering can enhance your social life and provide a sense of belonging. It also offers opportunities to collaborate on projects, share experiences, and make new friends.

Pursuing Causes: Creating Lasting Impact

In addition to volunteering, pursuing causes that align with your values can be a powerful way to create purpose and contribute to meaningful change. Here's how you can get involved in causes that matter to you:

1. Advocacy and Awareness

Consider becoming an advocate for causes that are important to you. This could involve raising awareness, participating in advocacy campaigns, or working with organizations to promote social or environmental change.

Advocacy can take many forms, from writing letters to legislators and organizing community events to participating in public demonstrations and using social media to raise awareness.

2. Philanthropy and Giving

Financial contributions and philanthropy are important ways to support causes you care about. Consider making donations to organizations or charities that align with your values.

You might also explore opportunities to set up a charitable fund or foundation, contribute to community projects, or support initiatives that address pressing social issues.

3. Community Involvement and Leadership

Take an active role in your community by participating in local boards, committees, or organizations. Community involvement allows you to contribute your skills and experience while making a positive impact on local issues.

Leadership roles within community organizations can provide additional opportunities for growth and contribution. Consider stepping into leadership positions that align with your interests and expertise.

4. Engaging with Global Issues

If you're interested in global issues, explore opportunities to engage with international organizations or initiatives. This might involve supporting global development projects, participating in international volunteer programs, or advocating for global causes.

Engaging with global issues allows you to contribute to meaningful change on a broader scale and connect with individuals and organizations working towards common goals.

Overcoming Challenges in Finding Purpose

Finding and creating purpose in retirement can come with its own set of challenges. Addressing these challenges proactively can help you stay motivated and engaged in meaningful activities.

1. Navigating Uncertainty

It's natural to experience uncertainty when transitioning into retirement and seeking new sources of purpose. Embrace this period of exploration and give yourself the time and space to discover what resonates with you.

Be open to trying new activities and adjusting your approach as needed. Remember that finding purpose is a journey, and it may take time to identify the activities and roles that bring you the most fulfillment.

2. Balancing Multiple Interests

Balancing multiple interests and activities can be challenging, especially if you're passionate about several causes or roles. Prioritize your commitments and set realistic goals to manage your time effectively.

Create a schedule that allows you to engage in a variety of activities while maintaining a sense of balance. It's important to allocate time for both personal pursuits and meaningful contributions.

3. Dealing with Setbacks

Setbacks and obstacles are a natural part of the process when creating purpose and pursuing new opportunities. Stay resilient and adaptable in the face of challenges.

Reflect on setbacks as learning experiences and adjust your approach as needed. Seek support from friends, mentors, or community resources to help you overcome obstacles and stay motivated.

LEGACY PLANNING

Legacy planning is an essential component of retirement, encompassing not only the distribution of your financial assets but also the transmission of your values, wisdom, and personal legacy.

The Concept of Legacy Planning

Legacy planning involves more than just preparing for the distribution of your assets. It is about shaping how you will be remembered and the values and impact you wish to leave behind. This process includes financial, emotional, and intellectual aspects, all of which contribute to the legacy you create.

A clear understanding of what you want your legacy to be is the foundation of effective legacy planning. Reflect on the values, experiences, and achievements that are most important to you and consider how you want these to be remembered by future generations.

Your legacy may encompass various elements, including financial assets, personal values, family traditions, and contributions to your community. Defining your legacy involves identifying what matters most to you and how you want to ensure that these aspects are preserved and passed on.

Retirement provides an ideal opportunity to focus on legacy planning, as you have the time and perspective to consider the impact you want to make. This period allows you to reflect on your life's achievements, values, and goals and to plan how to share these with your family and community.

Legacy planning in retirement involves not only financial considerations but also personal and emotional aspects. It is about creating a meaningful impact that extends beyond your lifetime and influences the lives of those you care about.

Preparing Your Estate

Estate planning is a critical component of legacy planning, ensuring that your financial assets are distributed according to your wishes and that your affairs are handled efficiently. Effective estate planning involves several key steps:

1. Creating a Will

A will is a legal document that outlines how your assets will be distributed upon your death. It is essential for ensuring that your wishes are followed and that your estate is managed according to your preferences.

In your will, you should specify how your assets, such as property, investments, and personal belongings, should be divided among your beneficiaries. You can also name an executor to manage your estate and ensure that your wishes are carried out.

Updating your will regularly is important to reflect changes in your circumstances, such as changes in family dynamics, financial situations, or new assets.

2. Establishing Trusts

Trusts are legal arrangements that allow you to transfer assets to a trustee who manages them on behalf of your beneficiaries. Trusts can be used to achieve various goals, including minimizing estate taxes, protecting assets from creditors, and ensuring that your assets are distributed according to your wishes.

Common types of trusts include revocable trusts, which can be modified or revoked during your lifetime, and irrevocable trusts, which cannot be altered once established. Trusts can also provide for specific conditions or purposes, such as funding educational expenses or supporting charitable causes.

3. Planning for Taxes

Effective estate planning involves strategies to minimize estate taxes and maximize the value of the assets passed on to your beneficiaries. Consider working with a tax advisor or estate planning attorney to develop strategies for minimizing tax liability.

Techniques such as gifting assets during your lifetime, establishing trusts, and taking advantage of tax exemptions can help reduce the impact of estate taxes on your estate. Proper planning can ensure that your beneficiaries receive the maximum benefit from your estate.

4. Designating Beneficiaries

Review and update beneficiary designations for assets such as life insurance policies, retirement accounts, and other financial accounts. Ensure that the beneficiaries listed on these accounts align with your overall estate planning goals.

It is important to coordinate beneficiary designations with the provisions of your will and trusts to avoid conflicts or unintended distributions. Regularly review these designations to ensure they reflect your current wishes.

5. Addressing Healthcare and End-of-Life Decisions

Estate planning also involves making decisions about healthcare and end-of-life care. Create advance directives, such as a living will or healthcare power of attorney, to specify your preferences for medical treatment and appoint someone to make healthcare decisions on your behalf if you become incapacitated.

Addressing these decisions in advance can ensure that your wishes are honored and provide peace of mind for both you and your loved ones.

Sharing Your Knowledge and Wisdom

In addition to financial planning, legacy planning involves passing on your knowledge, values, and experiences to future generations. Sharing your wisdom can have a profound impact on your family and community.

1. Documenting Your Life Story

Documenting your life story is a meaningful way to share your experiences, values, and lessons learned with future generations.

Consider writing an autobiography, recording personal stories, or creating a family history.

Sharing your life story provides valuable insights into your experiences and the values that have shaped your life. It also creates a lasting record that can be cherished and passed down through generations.

2. Creating Family Traditions and Values

Establishing and preserving family traditions and values is an important aspect of legacy planning. Consider creating traditions that reflect your values and cultural heritage and that can be continued by future generations.

Family traditions, such as holiday rituals, annual gatherings, or special celebrations, can help strengthen family bonds and create a sense of continuity. Sharing your values and traditions helps ensure that your legacy is honored and carried forward.

3. Mentoring and Teaching

Providing guidance and mentorship to younger family members or community members is a valuable way to share your knowledge and expertise. Consider offering mentorship in areas where you have experience and can provide valuable insights.

Teaching and mentoring can take many forms, from formal educational programs to informal conversations. Your guidance can have a lasting impact on others and contribute to their personal and professional growth.

4. Creating a Charitable Legacy

Consider establishing a charitable foundation or making contributions to causes that are important to you. Creating a charitable legacy allows you to support organizations and initiatives that align with your values and make a positive impact on your community.

Charitable giving can take various forms, including direct donations, setting up a donor-advised fund, or establishing a charitable trust. Your contributions can create lasting change and leave a meaningful legacy for future generations.

Communicating Your Legacy Plan

Effective legacy planning requires clear communication with your family and loved ones. Ensuring that your wishes are understood and that your plan is executed as intended involves several key steps:

1. Discussing Your Plans with Family

Open communication with your family about your legacy plans is crucial for avoiding misunderstandings and ensuring that your wishes are honored. Discuss your estate planning documents, charitable goals, and any specific instructions with your family members.

Address any questions or concerns they may have and provide guidance on how to manage and carry out your legacy plan. Clear communication helps prevent conflicts and ensures that everyone is aware of your intentions.

2. Documenting Your Wishes

Ensure that your legacy plan is documented and accessible to those who need to carry out your wishes. This includes providing copies of your will, trusts, and other estate planning documents to your executor, trustee, and family members.

Documenting your wishes also involves providing instructions for any specific requests or personal items that you want to be distributed according to your preferences.

3. Reviewing and Updating Your Plan

Regularly review and update your legacy plan to reflect changes in your circumstances, family dynamics, or financial situation. Ensure that your plan remains current and aligned with your goals.

Schedule periodic reviews with your estate planning attorney or financial advisor to make any necessary adjustments to your plan. Keeping your plan up to date ensures that it accurately reflects your wishes and remains effective.

EXPLORING THE WORLD IN RETIREMENT

Retirement offers a unique opportunity to explore the world, embrace new experiences, and fulfill a lifelong sense of adventure. With more time on your hands and fewer constraints, you can make travel and exploration a central part of your retirement lifestyle.

Travel in retirement is more than just a leisure activity; it's a way to enrich your life, discover new cultures, and create lasting memories. It allows you to break away from routine, challenge yourself, and engage with the world in new and meaningful ways.

The benefits of travel are numerous. It offers personal growth, mental stimulation, and improved well-being. Exploring new places and cultures broadens your horizons, stimulates creativity, and keeps your mind active. Additionally, it provides opportunities for relaxation, rejuvenation, and stress relief. Research indicates that travel enhances your overall quality of life by adding a sense of excitement and fulfillment. It encourages you to step out of your comfort zone, learn new skills, and engage in physical activities that promote health and vitality.

Finding your travel style is crucial. Retirement is an ideal time to discover and embrace the types of travel experiences that excite you the most. Whether you enjoy leisurely cruises, adventurous hikes, cultural immersions, or relaxing beach getaways, there are countless ways to explore the world that suit your interests and preferences. Reflecting on what appeals to you—whether it's structured tours, independent exploration, or a combination of both—will influence the destinations you choose and the activities you engage in.

Planning Your Travel Adventures

Effective planning is essential for making the most of your travel experiences. A well-thought-out plan can help you maximize your time, budget, and enjoyment.

Setting clear travel goals and priorities is the first step. Determine what you hope to achieve from your travels, whether it's exploring new destinations, experiencing different cultures, or pursuing specific activities. Creating a list of destinations and experiences you want to have can serve as a guide for planning your trips and help you prioritize the adventures that matter most to you.

Budgeting for travel is also crucial. Establishing a travel budget helps manage expenses and ensures you stay within your financial means. Include costs such as transportation, accommodation, meals, activities, and travel insurance. Creating a detailed budget for each trip and setting aside funds specifically for travel-related expenses can help you stay organized. Look for ways to save money by booking flights and accommodations in advance, taking advantage of discounts, and choosing budget-friendly options.

Researching destinations is another important aspect of travel planning. Consider factors such as climate, local customs, safety, and accessibility when choosing where to go. Use travel guides, online resources, and recommendations from friends and fellow travelers to gather information about your chosen destinations. This research will help you plan your itinerary and ensure you make the most of your time there.

Selecting the right accommodations can significantly impact your travel experience. Consider factors such as location, amenities, and cost when choosing where to stay. Explore various accommodation options, including hotels, vacation rentals, bed and breakfasts, and hostels. Look for accommodations that offer comfort, convenience, and good value for your money.

Creating a detailed itinerary helps you make the most of your travel time and ensures that you don't miss out on key attractions and activities. Plan your days in advance, but also allow for flexibility to explore spontaneously and relax. Include a mix of activities that align with your interests and goals, such as sightseeing, cultural experiences, outdoor adventures, and leisure time.

Exploring Local Travel Opportunities

While international travel offers exciting opportunities, exploring your local area can also provide rewarding and enriching experiences. Local travel allows you to discover hidden gems and appreciate the beauty and culture of your own region.

Discovering nearby destinations can be a great way to experience new places without the need for long-distance travel or extensive planning. Research nearby towns, natural parks, historical sites, and cultural attractions. Consider day trips or weekend getaways to explore these areas and immerse yourself in local experiences.

Participating in local events and festivals can provide unique and memorable experiences. Check local event calendars for opportunities to enjoy cultural celebrations, music festivals, food fairs, and community activities. Attending these events allows you to connect with your community, experience local traditions, and support local businesses and artists.

Engaging in outdoor activities is another way to enjoy local travel. Take advantage of outdoor activities and natural attractions in your area, such as hiking, biking, kayaking, and birdwatching. Exploring local parks, nature reserves, and scenic trails offers opportunities for adventure, tranquility, and appreciation of the natural world.

Supporting local businesses during your travels is important as well. When traveling locally, consider visiting small shops, restaurants, and markets to experience regional flavors and products. Supporting local businesses helps strengthen your community and fosters a sense of connection to the places you visit.

Embarking on International Travel Adventures

International travel provides opportunities to explore diverse cultures, landscapes, and experiences. Planning international trips requires additional considerations to ensure a smooth and enjoyable experience.

Understanding travel requirements is essential before traveling internationally. Research the entry requirements for your destination, including visa requirements, vaccinations, and travel advisories. Ensure that your passport is valid for the duration of your trip and meets the entry requirements of your destination. Check for any travel restrictions or safety concerns that may affect your plans, and stay informed about local laws and customs.

Navigating language and culture is an important aspect of international travel. Learning about the language and culture of your destination can enhance your travel experience and facilitate communication. Familiarize yourself with basic phrases and cultural norms to interact more effectively with locals. Consider taking a language course or using language translation apps to assist with communication. Understanding cultural customs and etiquette will help you navigate social interactions and show respect for local traditions.

Planning for health and safety is crucial when traveling internationally. Purchase travel insurance to cover medical emergencies, trip cancellations, and lost belongings. Take necessary health precautions, such as vaccinations and preventative measures for diseases common in your destination. Carry a first-aid kit and any necessary medications, and stay informed about health risks.

Managing currency and expenses is another important aspect of international travel. Understand the currency and financial practices of your destination, including exchange rates, payment methods, and budgeting for expenses. Consider using credit cards or travel money cards for convenience and security. Be aware of local banking practices and ensure you have access to funds for your trip.

To create a memorable international experience, immerse yourself in the local culture and engage in activities that resonate with you. Explore historical sites, try local cuisine, and interact with locals to gain a deeper understanding of your destination. Capture your experiences through photographs, journaling, or other creative means. Reflect on your adventures and share your stories with friends and family.

Staying Active and Healthy While Traveling

Maintaining your health and well-being while traveling is essential for enjoying your adventures to the fullest. Incorporate healthy habits into your travel routine to stay energized and comfortable.

Pay attention to your diet while traveling to ensure good health. Enjoy local cuisine, but also make an effort to incorporate balanced meals and nutritious snacks into your diet. Stay hydrated by drinking plenty of water, especially when traveling to high-altitude or hot climates. Be mindful of food safety and avoid consuming items that may cause digestive issues.

Incorporate physical activity into your travel routine to stay fit and energized. Engage in activities such as walking tours, hiking, or swimming while exploring new destinations. Many hotels and accommodations offer fitness facilities or access to local gyms. Consider incorporating exercise into your daily routine to maintain your health and well-being.

Ensure you get sufficient rest during your travels to avoid fatigue and maintain your energy levels. Prioritize quality sleep and allow time for relaxation between activities. Create a comfortable sleeping environment by bringing essential items such as travel pillows, earplugs, and eye masks. Follow a consistent sleep routine to help adjust to different time zones.

Travel can sometimes be stressful, especially when dealing with logistics and unexpected challenges. Practice stress-reduction techniques such as deep breathing, mindfulness, or meditation to stay calm and relaxed. Plan ahead to minimize stressors and allow for flexibility in your itinerary. Approach travel challenges with a positive mindset and view them as opportunities for growth and learning.

THE EMOTIONAL SIDE OF RETIREMENT

Retirement marks a significant transition in life, bringing about profound changes not just in daily routines but in emotional landscapes as well. As you move from a structured work life into the more fluid realm of retirement, you may encounter a range of emotional challenges. This chapter explores how to navigate these emotional aspects effectively, addressing common issues such as adjusting to a new identity, battling loneliness, and managing time effectively. By understanding and addressing these challenges, you can create a fulfilling and balanced retirement experience.

Adjusting to a New Identity

One of the most profound changes in retirement is the shift in personal identity. For many, work has been a central component of their identity and self-worth. The transition from being an active professional to a retiree can lead to a sense of loss and disorientation. The key to navigating this shift lies in redefining your identity and finding new sources of purpose and fulfillment.

Firstly, acknowledge and accept the emotions that come with this transition. It's natural to feel a sense of loss or confusion as you adjust to a new role. Give yourself time to adapt and reflect on how your identity is changing. Understand that retirement does not diminish your value or achievements; rather, it opens up opportunities to explore new interests and passions.

To redefine your identity, consider what aspects of your previous work life you enjoyed and how they might translate into your new life. Reflect on your skills, strengths, and interests, and think about how you can apply them in different ways. For example, if you enjoyed mentoring others, you might find fulfillment in volunteering or part-time work that allows you to share your expertise.

Explore new roles and activities that can help shape your new identity. Engage in hobbies, take up new interests, or pursue educational opportunities. Setting new goals and challenges can provide a sense of direction and accomplishment. Whether it's learning a new skill, starting a new project, or engaging in community activities, these experiences can help you build a new sense of purpose and identity.

Battling Loneliness and Building Social Connections

Loneliness is a common emotional challenge in retirement, particularly for those who have spent much of their life in a busy work environment surrounded by colleagues. The absence of daily social interactions can lead to feelings of isolation and loneliness. Addressing this issue involves proactive steps to build and maintain meaningful social connections.

Start by reaching out to family and friends. Maintain regular contact with loved ones through phone calls, video chats, or visits. Reconnecting with old friends or expanding your social circle can help reduce feelings of isolation. Make an effort to stay engaged with people who bring positivity and support into your life.

Consider joining social or community groups that align with your interests. Many retirement communities and local organizations offer activities and clubs that provide opportunities to meet new people. Whether it's a book club, a gardening group, or a fitness class, participating in these activities can help you build new friendships and stay socially active.

Volunteering is another excellent way to combat loneliness. Engaging in volunteer work not only provides a sense of purpose but also connects you with others who share your interests and values. Look for volunteer opportunities in areas you are passionate about, such as education, healthcare, or environmental conservation. Volunteering can enrich your life and provide a sense of community and belonging.

Incorporate social activities into your routine. Schedule regular outings, social gatherings, or group activities to stay engaged with others. Setting aside time for social interactions can help you maintain connections and create new ones. Consider exploring new interests or hobbies that involve group participation, such as joining a local sports league or attending cultural events.

Managing Time Effectively

The transition from a structured work schedule to the unstructured time of retirement can be challenging. Without the framework of work-related tasks and deadlines, you may find yourself struggling with time management. Effectively managing your time is crucial for maintaining a sense of purpose and achieving a balanced lifestyle.

Start by establishing a routine. While retirement offers flexibility, having a daily or weekly routine can provide structure and a sense of normalcy. Plan your days to include a mix of activities that reflect your interests and priorities. Create a schedule that incorporates exercise, hobbies, social interactions, and relaxation.

Setting goals and priorities is essential for effective time management. Identify what you want to achieve in retirement and set specific, achievable goals. Whether it's completing a personal project, traveling, or pursuing a new interest, having clear goals can help you stay motivated and focused. Break down larger goals into smaller, manageable tasks and create a timeline for accomplishing them.

Time management tools and techniques can also be helpful. Use planners, calendars, or digital tools to organize your schedule and keep track of commitments. Set reminders for important tasks and activities to stay on track. Prioritize tasks based on their importance and deadlines, and be flexible in adjusting your schedule as needed.

Balance is key to effective time management. Ensure that your schedule includes a mix of productive activities, leisure time, and self-care. Avoid overloading yourself with too many commitments and allow time for relaxation and spontaneous activities. Finding the right balance will help you maintain a sense of fulfillment and well-being.

Coping with Changes in Relationships

Retirement can also impact your relationships, both positively and negatively. As you transition into retirement, you may experience changes in your interactions with family and friends. Navigating these changes requires open communication and adaptability.

Discuss your retirement plans and expectations with your family. Share your thoughts and feelings about the changes you're experiencing and listen to their perspectives. Open communication can help manage expectations and address any concerns or adjustments that may arise.

Be mindful of how your retirement may affect your relationships. Spending more time at home may alter dynamics with your partner or family members. Make an effort to maintain a healthy balance between your personal activities and family time. Communicate openly with your loved ones about your needs and interests, and work together to find solutions that support each other's well-being.

Foster new relationships and connections outside of your immediate family. Engage in social activities, join community groups, or participate in local events to expand your social network. Building new friendships and connections can provide additional sources of support and companionship.

Finding Support and Resources

Navigating the emotional side of retirement can be challenging, but there are resources available to support you through this transition. Seeking professional help or joining support groups can provide valuable guidance and assistance.

Consider consulting with a therapist or counselor who specializes in retirement or life transitions. A mental health professional can help you address any emotional challenges, provide coping strategies, and support you in adjusting to your new lifestyle.

Explore support groups or workshops focused on retirement and aging. These groups can provide opportunities to connect with others who are experiencing similar challenges and share insights and strategies. Participating in support groups can help you feel less isolated and provide a sense of community.

Many communities offer resources and programs for retirees, including educational workshops, social activities, and health services. Take advantage of these resources to enhance your retirement experience and stay informed about available support.

Embracing a Positive Outlook

Maintaining a positive outlook is crucial for navigating the emotional side of retirement. Embrace this new chapter of your life with an open mind and a willingness to explore new opportunities. Focus on the aspects of retirement that bring you joy and fulfillment, and approach challenges with resilience and optimism.

Practice self-care and prioritize activities that contribute to your well-being. Engage in activities that bring you happiness, whether it's pursuing hobbies, spending time with loved ones, or engaging in creative projects. Cultivate a mindset of gratitude and appreciation for the opportunities and experiences that retirement offers.

Set realistic expectations and be patient with yourself as you adjust to retirement. Recognize that the transition may take time and that it's normal to experience a range of emotions. Allow yourself to adapt at your own pace and seek support when needed.

MASTERING TIME

Retirement offers an unparalleled freedom to shape your days as you see fit, but with this freedom comes the challenge of structuring your time effectively. Crafting a balanced schedule that incorporates relaxation, productivity, and personal growth is essential for a fulfilling retirement.

The Importance of Structure

While retirement liberates you from the constraints of a work schedule, it can also lead to a lack of structure that may leave you feeling unfulfilled or aimless. A well-structured day provides a sense of routine, helps maintain a healthy balance, and promotes overall well-being. Establishing a daily schedule can create a sense of normalcy and purpose, reducing stress and enhancing your quality of life.

Effective time management in retirement involves finding a balance between productive activities, relaxation, and personal growth. This balance allows you to enjoy the freedom of retirement while also staying engaged and motivated. A structured schedule helps you make the most of your time, achieve your goals, and maintain a sense of achievement and satisfaction.

Creating a Balanced Schedule

The foundation of a fulfilling retirement schedule lies in creating a balance between different aspects of your life. A balanced schedule includes time for relaxation, productivity, and personal growth, ensuring that you address all areas of your well-being.

1. Incorporating Relaxation

Relaxation is a crucial component of a balanced retirement schedule. It allows you to recharge, reduce stress, and enjoy the fruits of your labor. To incorporate relaxation effectively, allocate dedicated time for activities that help you unwind and rejuvenate.

Begin by identifying activities that help you relax and bring you joy. These might include reading, gardening, listening to music, or simply enjoying nature. Schedule regular periods of downtime throughout your week to engage in these activities. For example, you might set aside an hour each afternoon for reading or take a leisurely walk in the evening.

Consider creating relaxation rituals that signal the end of your day. This could involve activities such as meditating, practicing yoga, or enjoying a warm bath. Establishing a routine that helps you unwind before bedtime can improve your sleep quality and overall well-being.

In addition to daily relaxation, plan for periodic getaways or mini-vacations. Taking breaks from your routine can provide a refreshing change of pace and allow you to explore new environments. Whether it's a weekend trip to a nearby town or a longer vacation, time away from home can enhance your sense of relaxation and enjoyment.

2. Fostering Productivity

Maintaining productivity in retirement provides a sense of purpose and accomplishment. While you may no longer have work-related tasks, there are plenty of opportunities to stay productive and engaged. Setting goals and pursuing meaningful activities can contribute to a fulfilling retirement experience.

Start by identifying areas of interest or projects you'd like to pursue. This could include hobbies, volunteering, or personal projects. Create a list of goals and tasks related to these interests and incorporate them into your schedule. For instance, if you enjoy woodworking, allocate time each week to work on projects or join a woodworking club.

Consider taking on part-time work or consulting opportunities if you desire continued professional engagement. Part-time work allows you to stay active in your field while also providing additional income. Consulting or freelance work can offer flexibility and the opportunity to use your skills and experience in new ways.

Develop a daily or weekly to-do list to keep track of your tasks and priorities. This helps you stay organized and ensures that you address important activities. Break larger projects into smaller, manageable tasks and set deadlines to stay on track. Regularly review your progress and adjust your schedule as needed.

3. Promoting Personal Growth

Retirement is an ideal time for personal growth and exploration. With fewer responsibilities, you have the freedom to pursue new interests, learn new skills, and engage in activities that enrich your life. Incorporating personal growth into your schedule enhances your overall sense of fulfillment and satisfaction.

Identify areas of interest or goals you'd like to pursue. This might include learning a new language, taking up a new hobby, or pursuing educational opportunities. Set aside time each week for personal development activities. For example, you might schedule a weekly language class or dedicate time to practicing a new skill.

Consider exploring new experiences and stepping out of your comfort zone. Travel, attend workshops, or join groups related to your interests. Engaging in new experiences can broaden your horizons, stimulate your mind, and provide a sense of adventure.

Incorporate reflection and goal-setting into your schedule. Regularly assess your progress and adjust your goals as needed. This reflection allows you to stay focused on your personal growth journey and make adjustments to your schedule to align with your evolving interests and aspirations.

Time Management Strategies

Effectively managing your time in retirement involves implementing strategies that help you stay organized, focused, and balanced. By adopting these strategies, you can create a schedule that enhances your overall well-being and ensures that you make the most of your retirement years.

1. Prioritization

Prioritizing tasks and activities is essential for effective time management. Start by identifying your most important and meaningful activities. Focus on these priorities and allocate time in your schedule accordingly. Avoid getting caught up in less important tasks that may distract you from your core goals and interests.

Use tools such as to-do lists or planners to organize your tasks and set priorities. Break tasks into smaller, manageable steps and tackle them based on their importance and deadlines. Regularly review your priorities and adjust your schedule to ensure you stay on track.

2. Scheduling

Creating a detailed schedule helps you allocate time for various activities and maintain a sense of structure. Plan your days or weeks in advance, including time for relaxation, productivity, and personal growth. Consider using a calendar or digital scheduling tool to keep track of your commitments and activities.

Include buffer time in your schedule to account for unexpected events or changes. Flexibility is key to managing your time effectively and adapting to unforeseen circumstances. Allow room for spontaneity and leisure, ensuring that your schedule remains balanced and enjoyable.

3. Time Blocking

Time blocking is a time management technique that involves allocating specific blocks of time for different activities. By designating time blocks for tasks, you can stay focused and avoid multitasking. For example, you might set aside a block of time each morning for personal projects and another block in the afternoon for relaxation.

Time blocking helps you create a structured routine and ensures that you allocate sufficient time for each activity. It also helps prevent procrastination and improves productivity by providing clear timeframes for completing tasks.

4. Avoiding Overcommitment

Avoiding overcommitment is crucial for maintaining a balanced schedule. Be mindful of how much you take on and ensure that your commitments align with your priorities and interests. Overcommitting can lead to stress and burnout, detracting from the enjoyment of your retirement.

Learn to say no to activities or commitments that do not align with your goals or values. Prioritize activities that bring you joy and fulfillment, and be selective about additional commitments. Allow yourself time to relax and enjoy your retirement without feeling overwhelmed.

5. Maintaining Flexibility

While having a structured schedule is important, maintaining flexibility is equally crucial. Life is unpredictable, and unexpected events or changes may arise. Be prepared to adjust your schedule as needed and adapt to new circumstances.

Embrace a mindset of adaptability and openness to change. Allow room for spontaneity and unplanned activities that may arise. Flexibility ensures that you remain engaged and responsive to opportunities and challenges, enhancing your overall experience of retirement.

Balancing Routine and Spontaneity

Finding the right balance between routine and spontaneity is essential for a fulfilling retirement. A structured routine provides a sense of stability and purpose, while spontaneity adds excitement and variety to your life.

Incorporate elements of routine into your daily life to establish a sense of structure and normalcy. This might include regular exercise, mealtimes, or designated periods for relaxation and productivity. A consistent routine helps you maintain healthy habits and stay organized.

At the same time, allow space for spontaneous activities and adventures. Embrace opportunities that arise unexpectedly and be open to trying new experiences. Spontaneity adds an element of excitement and creativity to your life, keeping your retirement engaging and enjoyable.

Evaluating and Adjusting Your Schedule

Regularly evaluating and adjusting your schedule is essential for ensuring that it continues to meet your needs and goals. Reflect on your experiences and assess how well your schedule aligns with your priorities and interests.

Take time to review your schedule periodically, such as monthly or quarterly. Assess what is working well and identify areas for improvement. Make adjustments based on your evolving interests, goals, and lifestyle changes.

Seek feedback from family and friends if needed. They can provide valuable insights and perspectives on how your schedule impacts your overall well-being and relationships. Use their feedback to make informed adjustments and enhance your retirement experience.

THE GOLDEN YEARS

Retirement is often envisioned as the "golden years"—a time of relaxation, freedom, and fulfillment. To truly realize this ideal, however, one must adopt a holistic approach that integrates financial health, emotional well-being, and lasting happiness.

Financial Health: The Foundation of a Fulfilling Retirement

Financial security is the cornerstone of a successful retirement. While it provides peace of mind, it's essential to recognize that financial stability alone does not guarantee fulfillment. For a truly enriching retirement, financial health must be complemented by emotional well-being and personal satisfaction.

To start, crafting a comprehensive financial plan is crucial. Begin by evaluating your current financial status—assets, liabilities, income sources, and expenses. Creating a budget that reflects your retirement goals and lifestyle aspirations is a vital first step. Ensure that your budget covers projected healthcare costs, travel plans, and any other activities you intend to pursue.

Working with a financial advisor can greatly enhance your planning process. An advisor can help optimize your investment portfolio, plan for taxes, and develop strategies for managing your wealth throughout retirement. Regularly reviewing and adjusting your financial plan is important as your circumstances and goals evolve.

Beyond traditional savings and investments, consider diversifying your income streams. This might include exploring options like annuities, rental properties, or part-time work.

Diversification not only provides additional security but also offers greater flexibility, allowing you to fully enjoy your retirement.

Healthcare costs represent a significant aspect of retirement planning. With medical expenses often rising, having a well-thought-out plan for managing these costs is essential. Understanding your options for health insurance, including Medicare and supplemental plans, can help you navigate the complexities of healthcare coverage. Additionally, setting up a Health Savings Account (HSA) can offer tax benefits for medical expenses, while long-term care insurance can protect you against the high costs of extended care or assisted living.

Maintaining a flexible budget is also key. Regularly reviewing your expenses and income will help ensure that your budget remains aligned with your needs and goals. Incorporating a contingency fund into your budget can help cover unexpected costs or emergencies, providing an extra layer of financial security.

Emotional Well-Being: Nurturing Your Inner Self

Emotional well-being plays a crucial role in a happy and fulfilling retirement. The transition from a structured work life to retirement can evoke a range of emotions, from excitement to anxiety. Nurturing your emotional health involves acknowledging these feelings, finding new sources of joy, and maintaining meaningful connections.

Embracing the changes that come with retirement is essential. Recognize that retirement brings significant shifts in your daily routine and identity. Accept any feelings of loss or uncertainty, and give yourself time to adjust to your new lifestyle. Setting realistic expectations and approaching retirement with a positive outlook will help you navigate this transition more smoothly.

Cultivating new interests and hobbies is vital for emotional well-being. Engage in activities that bring you joy and stimulate your mind. Whether it's learning a new skill, pursuing a creative project, or participating in a sport, finding activities that resonate with you can enhance your sense of purpose and satisfaction. Joining clubs, groups, or classes related to your interests can also provide valuable social connections and enrich your retirement experience.

Prioritizing mental health and self-care is equally important. Incorporate practices that promote relaxation, mindfulness, and stress reduction into your daily routine. Activities such as meditation, yoga, or journaling can help manage stress and maintain a positive outlook. Seeking professional help, if needed, can also provide support for managing emotions and addressing any mental health concerns.

Lasting Happiness: Creating a Meaningful and Joyful Retirement

True happiness in retirement comes from creating a life that aligns with your values, goals, and aspirations. It involves finding meaning, building connections, and embracing the opportunities that retirement offers.

A sense of purpose is fundamental to lasting happiness. Identify activities and pursuits that provide meaning and satisfaction. This could include volunteering, mentoring, or pursuing a long-held dream. Engaging in purposeful activities enhances your sense of fulfillment and contributes to a meaningful retirement. Setting personal goals that align with your passions and values provides direction and motivation, allowing you to stay focused on what truly matters to you.

Building and maintaining strong relationships is crucial for happiness. Nurture existing connections with family and friends, and make an effort to forge new ones. Regular social interactions provide emotional support, companionship, and a sense of community. Engaging in activities that facilitate social interactions, such as joining clubs or attending events, helps maintain a vibrant social network.

Embracing life's adventures adds excitement and joy to your retirement. Travel, explore new places, and take on challenges that inspire you. Whether it's a long-awaited trip, a new hobby, or a spontaneous adventure, these experiences contribute to a rich and fulfilling retirement. Balance adventurous pursuits with relaxation and downtime to maintain a harmonious and enjoyable retirement experience.

Regularly reflecting on your retirement experience and making adjustments as needed is also important. Assess what aspects of your life are working well and identify areas for improvement. Reflection helps you stay aligned with your goals and ensures that you continue to find happiness and fulfillment. Being open to change and adapting your plans based on evolving interests and circumstances allows you to respond to new opportunities and challenges effectively.

PROTECTING YOUR WEALTH

As you move into retirement, protecting your wealth becomes a critical aspect of ensuring long-term financial stability. Your retirement savings must withstand the challenges of inflation, market fluctuations, and unexpected expenses to provide you with the security and peace of mind you need. This chapter delves into strategies for shielding your retirement savings from these risks, ensuring that your financial resources remain intact and capable of supporting your desired lifestyle.

Understanding the Risks

Inflation is one of the most significant threats to your retirement savings. Over time, inflation erodes the purchasing power of your money, meaning that what you could buy with a certain amount of money today will cost more in the future. For retirees, this means that the income you rely on to cover your expenses may not stretch as far as it did when you first retired.

Market risks also pose a threat. Financial markets are inherently volatile, and economic downturns can lead to significant declines in investment values. Such fluctuations can impact your retirement portfolio, especially if a substantial portion of your savings is invested in the stock market or other volatile assets.

Unexpected expenses can further strain your finances. Life is unpredictable, and unexpected costs such as medical emergencies, home repairs, or other unforeseen events can arise, potentially derailing your financial plans.

Strategies to Safeguard Against Inflation

1. Investing in Inflation-Protected Securities

One effective way to protect your retirement savings from inflation is to invest in inflation-protected securities. In the United States, Treasury Inflation-Protected Securities (TIPS) are a popular choice. These government bonds are designed to increase in value with inflation and decrease when inflation falls. They provide a guaranteed return that adjusts with inflation, helping to preserve your purchasing power.

2. Diversifying Your Investment Portfolio

Diversification is a key strategy for managing inflation risk. By spreading your investments across various asset classes—such as stocks, bonds, real estate, and commodities—you can reduce the impact of inflation on your portfolio. Stocks, for example, have historically provided returns that outpace inflation over the long term. Real estate investments can also offer protection against inflation, as property values and rental income often rise with inflation.

3. Incorporating Growth-Oriented Investments

While preserving capital is important, including growth-oriented investments in your portfolio can help offset the effects of inflation. Stocks, mutual funds, and exchange-traded funds (ETFs) that focus on growth can offer higher returns that potentially exceed the rate of inflation. It's crucial to balance these investments with more stable, income-generating assets to manage risk.

4. Adjusting Your Withdrawal Strategy

Your withdrawal strategy can also impact how well your savings withstand inflation. Using a dynamic withdrawal strategy, where you adjust your withdrawals based on inflation and market performance, can help preserve your savings. Instead of withdrawing a fixed amount annually, consider adjusting your withdrawals to keep pace with inflation, ensuring that your purchasing power remains stable.

Strategies to Protect Against Market Risks

1. Creating a Diversified Portfolio

Diversification is one of the most effective ways to mitigate market risk. By spreading your investments across different asset classes, industries, and geographical regions, you can reduce the overall risk of your portfolio. For example, investing in a mix of domestic and international stocks, bonds, and real estate can help buffer against market volatility and economic downturns.

2. Implementing a Safe Withdrawal Rate

A safe withdrawal rate is a critical component of managing market risk. The 4% rule is a commonly used guideline, suggesting that you withdraw 4% of your retirement savings annually. This rule is based on historical data indicating that a 4% withdrawal rate is likely to ensure that your savings last for a typical 30-year retirement. However, individual circumstances vary, so it's essential to tailor your withdrawal strategy based on your specific financial situation and market conditions.

3. Maintaining an Emergency Fund

An emergency fund is a crucial safeguard against unexpected expenses and market volatility. Keeping a portion of your savings in liquid, low-risk investments such as a high-yield savings account or short-term certificates of deposit (CDs) provides you with immediate access to funds in case of emergencies. Aim to have enough in your emergency fund to cover at least six months' worth of expenses.

4. Using Annuities for Guaranteed Income

Annuities can provide a reliable source of guaranteed income, helping to protect against market risks. Immediate annuities and fixed annuities offer regular payments for a specified period or for the rest of your life. This predictable income stream can help cover essential expenses, providing a buffer against market fluctuations and economic downturns.

Strategies to Handle Unexpected Expenses

1. Planning for Healthcare Costs

Healthcare costs are a significant potential expense in retirement. To manage this risk, consider purchasing long-term care insurance, which can help cover the costs of extended care services. Additionally, maintaining a Health Savings Account (HSA) or a similar tax-advantaged savings account can provide funds specifically earmarked for medical expenses.

2. Regularly Reviewing Your Financial Plan

Regularly reviewing and updating your financial plan is essential for managing unexpected expenses. Reassess your budget, expenses, and income sources periodically to ensure that your plan remains aligned with your current needs and circumstances. Adjustments may be necessary to accommodate changes in your health, lifestyle, or financial situation.

3. Exploring Alternative Income Sources

Having multiple income sources can help mitigate the impact of unexpected expenses. Consider options such as part-time work, rental income, or freelance opportunities to supplement your retirement savings. Diversifying your income streams provides additional security and flexibility in the face of unforeseen costs.

4. Establishing a Contingency Fund

A contingency fund is an extra reserve of money set aside to cover unexpected expenses. This fund should be separate from your emergency fund and invested in a low-risk, easily accessible account. By having a contingency fund, you can address unexpected costs without disrupting your primary retirement savings or investment strategy.

Safeguarding your retirement savings against inflation, market risks, and unexpected expenses is essential for maintaining long-term financial stability. By implementing strategies such as investing in inflation-protected securities, diversifying your portfolio, creating a safe withdrawal rate, and maintaining an emergency fund, you can protect your wealth and ensure that your retirement years are secure and enjoyable.

Planning for healthcare costs, regularly reviewing your financial plan, and exploring alternative income sources further enhance your ability to manage unexpected expenses. Adopting a holistic approach to wealth protection helps you navigate the complexities of retirement with confidence, allowing you to focus on enjoying the fruits of your labor.

In essence, protecting your wealth in retirement involves a combination of prudent financial planning, strategic investments, and proactive management of risks. By taking these steps, you can shield your savings from potential threats and create a secure foundation for a fulfilling retirement.

DOWNSIZING AND SIMPLIFYING

Retirement presents an opportunity to reflect on the things that truly matter and reassess how we approach our day-to-day lives. For many, this time marks a significant transition, not just financially but also in terms of lifestyle and priorities. One of the most impactful shifts that people make during this period is downsizing and simplifying their lives. This involves reducing expenses, streamlining possessions, and creating a lifestyle that aligns with your new goals and values.

Downsizing doesn't simply mean moving into a smaller home; it's about cultivating a life that fits your current needs and aspirations. It's about letting go of the excess, reducing complexities, and fostering an environment that promotes peace, contentment, and fulfillment. For many, this can mean selling a large family home that's no longer needed, decluttering accumulated possessions, or cutting down on expenses that no longer serve a purpose.

Shifting Priorities in Retirement

As we age, our priorities evolve. The hustle of building a career, raising children, and achieving milestones begins to quiet, and other aspects of life come into sharper focus. For many retirees, the desire for simplicity becomes paramount. Where once you might have been focused on accumulating wealth, material possessions, and achievements, retirement often brings a shift toward valuing time, experiences, and personal growth.

One of the key motivators for downsizing in retirement is the realization that you no longer need the same space or belongings that were once essential. Children may have grown and moved out, making a large family home feel empty and unnecessary. The pressures of maintaining a big house, from cleaning to paying utilities, may become more burdensome than rewarding. Additionally, the desire for mobility—whether it's to travel, live closer to loved ones, or enjoy a more relaxed lifestyle—can make maintaining a large property less appealing.

In retirement, simplifying becomes less about financial necessity and more about lifestyle choices. It's an opportunity to focus on what truly brings joy and fulfillment, cutting out the distractions and burdens that no longer serve your well-being.

Emotional Aspects of Downsizing

While downsizing can bring numerous benefits, it is not always an easy decision, especially when it comes to letting go of a home filled with memories or possessions that hold sentimental value. These emotional attachments can make the process challenging, but they are also an essential part of the journey toward simplicity.

One of the most common emotional hurdles in downsizing is the feeling of loss. Whether it's the family home you've lived in for decades, items you've collected over the years, or simply the lifestyle you've become accustomed to, downsizing can feel like letting go of a part of your identity. Acknowledging these emotions is crucial, and it's important to give yourself the time and space to process them.

However, it's also valuable to reframe the process. Downsizing doesn't mean losing something; it's about creating space for something new. By letting go of what no longer serves you, you open up opportunities for new experiences, relationships, and personal growth. You're not abandoning your past but rather distilling it down to the most important aspects, allowing them to shine more brightly in your life.

Simplifying your living situation can also provide a sense of liberation. As the burdens of maintaining a large home or managing excessive belongings are lifted, many retirees report feeling lighter and more focused. This newfound freedom allows you to devote more time and energy to activities and people that matter most.

Financial Benefits of Downsizing

From a financial perspective, downsizing can be a smart move in retirement. Reducing the size of your home or moving to a less expensive area can free up equity that you can reinvest into your retirement savings or use to fund other important goals, such as travel, hobbies, or helping family members. It can also reduce ongoing costs, such as property taxes, utilities, maintenance, and insurance.

For retirees who are concerned about their long-term financial stability, downsizing can provide a significant boost to their nest egg. Selling a large home and purchasing a smaller, more affordable property can leave you with extra cash that can be used for investments or to bolster your emergency fund. Alternatively, some retirees choose to rent instead of buying a new home, which can provide more flexibility and fewer financial obligations.

In addition to freeing up cash, downsizing can reduce the cost of home maintenance and upkeep. A smaller home generally requires less work to maintain, meaning fewer expenses for repairs, renovations, and routine upkeep. This not only saves money but also reduces the amount of time and effort you need to spend on household chores, giving you more freedom to enjoy your retirement.

Moreover, many retirees choose to relocate to areas with a lower cost of living, where housing and other expenses are more affordable. This can further stretch your retirement savings and allow you to live more comfortably without worrying about running out of money. By carefully planning your downsizing strategy, you can create a more sustainable and financially secure retirement lifestyle.

Practical Considerations for Downsizing

When it comes to the practical aspects of downsizing, the first step is to assess your current living situation and determine what changes will best support your retirement goals. This involves taking a close look at your home, your possessions, and your daily expenses to identify areas where you can simplify and streamline.

One of the most significant decisions retirees face is whether to stay in their current home or move to a smaller one. If you choose to stay in your home, you may still want to simplify your living environment by decluttering and reducing unnecessary possessions. This can make your home easier to manage and create a more peaceful and organized space.

If you decide to move, consider what type of home will best suit your needs in retirement. Many retirees opt for smaller homes or condos that require less maintenance and are easier to manage. Others may choose to move to a retirement community, where amenities and services such as landscaping, housekeeping, and security are provided, allowing them to focus on enjoying their retirement years without the burdens of homeownership.

When choosing a new home, consider factors such as proximity to family, healthcare facilities, and recreational activities. You'll also want to think about your long-term needs—such as accessibility and mobility—especially if you plan to age in place. Choosing a home that can accommodate potential future health challenges, such as single-level living or a home with accessibility features, can save you the hassle and cost of having to move again later in life.

Another practical consideration is the process of decluttering and downsizing your belongings. Start by sorting through your possessions and deciding what to keep, donate, sell, or discard. This can be a time-consuming and emotional process, so it's important to start early and take it one step at a time. Enlisting the help of family members or professional organizers can make the process easier and less overwhelming.

Focusing on What Matters Most

Ultimately, the goal of downsizing and simplifying in retirement is to create a lifestyle that aligns with your values and priorities. By reducing the physical, emotional, and financial burdens of excess, you can focus on what truly matters—whether that's spending time with loved ones, pursuing hobbies and interests, or simply enjoying the peace and contentment that comes with a simpler life.

Simplifying your life in retirement allows you to live with greater intentionality. Instead of being weighed down by the responsibilities of maintaining a large home or managing excessive possessions, you can devote your time and energy to the things that bring you joy and fulfillment. Whether it's traveling, volunteering, or simply enjoying the quiet moments of daily life, downsizing and simplifying create space for a more meaningful and satisfying retirement.

In conclusion, downsizing and simplifying are not just about reducing expenses or cutting back on material possessions; they are about creating a life that fits your current needs and aspirations. By embracing this process, you can set yourself up for a more fulfilling, financially secure, and purposeful retirement.

20 PROVEN STRATEGIES FOR LASTING WEALTH, HAPPINESS, AND FULFILLMENT

Retirement is not just the culmination of your working years but also the beginning of a new, vibrant chapter of life. It's an opportunity to enjoy the fruits of your labor, explore new interests, and foster deep fulfillment. However, achieving long-term wealth and happiness in retirement requires careful planning and a thoughtful approach. This chapter will explore 20 detailed strategies that will help you navigate retirement with confidence, ensuring lasting wealth, emotional well-being, and personal fulfillment.

1. Create a Comprehensive Financial Roadmap

The foundation of a successful retirement begins with a clear and comprehensive financial roadmap. This is not just a one-time budget plan but a dynamic strategy that guides your financial decisions over time. Start by identifying your retirement goals: how much income you'll need, where you want to live, and what lifestyle you aim to maintain. Factor in inflation, healthcare expenses, and any long-term care costs. By laying out these details, you create a pathway that gives you clarity and control over your finances, ensuring that unexpected expenses don't derail your plans. Consulting with a financial advisor is crucial in this stage to help craft a plan that is realistic and adaptable to changes in economic conditions.

2. Optimize Social Security Benefits

Many retirees claim Social Security benefits too early, unaware of the long-term impact on their financial security. Timing is everything with Social Security. If you can wait until your full retirement age (or even later, up to age 70), your monthly benefit increases substantially. This decision can provide thousands more in lifetime benefits, ensuring a more secure financial cushion in later years. However, the optimal age to claim varies based on factors such as your health, life expectancy, and overall retirement income. A strategic approach to Social Security maximizes this key income stream, contributing significantly to your financial longevity.

3. Diversify Income Streams

Depending solely on one source of income can leave you vulnerable to economic downturns or unforeseen events. Diversifying your income streams ensures that you are not placing all your financial eggs in one basket. This can include a mix of pensions, investment returns, rental income, part-time work, and Social Security. Building multiple income streams also gives you flexibility and freedom, allowing you to adjust to financial challenges without sacrificing your lifestyle. Consider the role of annuities, dividend-paying stocks, and even passive income sources such as online businesses or royalties as part of this strategy.

4. Eliminate High-Interest Debt Before Retirement

Debt, especially high-interest debt, can erode your financial security in retirement. Before you retire, it's essential to focus on paying off credit card balances, car loans, or other high-interest liabilities. Entering retirement debt-free allows you to reduce monthly expenses and keeps more of your income available for enjoying life, rather than funneling it toward interest payments. If you have a mortgage, carefully consider whether paying it off is the best financial move; in some cases, it may be advantageous, while in others, low-interest mortgage debt can be managed strategically.

5. Shift to Low-Risk Investments

As you approach or enter retirement, your investment strategy should shift from high-risk, high-reward assets to more stable, lower-risk options. The stock market's volatility can be a danger to retirees relying on their portfolio for income. Consider shifting a portion of your investments into bonds, certificates of deposit (CDs), or dividend-paying stocks that provide steady income with lower risk. While returns might be more modest, the goal here is capital preservation and stability, ensuring your savings last throughout your retirement years.

6. Regularly Rebalance Your Portfolio

Even in retirement, your investment portfolio requires regular attention and adjustments. Over time, market fluctuations can cause your asset allocation to drift from your original plan. Rebalancing ensures that your portfolio stays aligned with your risk tolerance and financial goals. For example, if the stock portion of your portfolio grows significantly, it may expose you to more risk than you intended. Regular rebalancing allows you to sell high-performing assets and buy lower-priced ones, keeping your portfolio healthy and within your comfort zone.

7. Cut Unnecessary Expenses

Living within your means in retirement is key to maintaining financial security. Take time to evaluate your spending habits and identify areas where you can cut back without sacrificing quality of life. Are there subscriptions, memberships, or services you no longer use? Is dining out or entertainment taking a larger chunk of your budget than necessary? Cutting these unnecessary expenses can free up money for travel, hobbies, or other fulfilling experiences. Living a more frugal lifestyle doesn't mean depriving yourself; it's about making smart choices that align with your retirement goals.

8. Create a Dedicated Healthcare Fund

Healthcare is one of the largest expenses retirees face, and it's often unpredictable. Setting aside a dedicated fund for medical expenses can help you avoid dipping into your primary savings or investments. Consider the potential costs of long-term care, prescription medications, surgeries, and regular medical check-ups. It's also wise to explore supplemental insurance options beyond Medicare to cover gaps in coverage. By preparing for these costs in advance, you protect your financial plan from being derailed by unforeseen medical emergencies.

9. Prioritize Physical Health

Physical well-being is foundational to a happy and fulfilling retirement. Staying physically active helps reduce healthcare costs, improves mental clarity, and allows you to fully engage in life's adventures. Developing a consistent exercise routine, whether it's walking, swimming, or yoga, will keep you strong and energetic. Consider activities that you enjoy so that fitness becomes a natural part of your day, not a chore. Staying active also combats chronic illnesses such as heart disease, diabetes, and arthritis, contributing to a longer, healthier life.

10. Engage in Lifelong Learning

Lifelong learning doesn't just keep your mind sharp; it also provides a sense of purpose and fulfillment. In retirement, you have the freedom to explore new interests, take up hobbies, or study subjects you've always been curious about. Whether through online courses, community college classes, or local workshops, continuous learning fosters intellectual growth and keeps you engaged with the world around you. This mental stimulation is crucial for combating cognitive decline and maintaining a youthful outlook on life.

11. Foster Strong Personal Relationships

Social connections are vital to emotional well-being, especially in retirement when the structure of daily work routines is gone. Nurturing relationships with family, friends, and your community gives you a support system that enriches life. Maintaining a regular social schedule, whether through gatherings, phone calls, or online chats, prevents feelings of isolation and loneliness, which can negatively affect both mental and physical health. Consider joining clubs, participating in group activities, or even starting a new hobby with others to expand your social network.

12. Volunteer or Mentor

Giving back is one of the most fulfilling ways to spend your retirement. Volunteering for causes you care about or mentoring younger generations allows you to share your wisdom and skills, making a lasting impact on others. This contribution of time and knowledge not only benefits the community but also gives you a deep sense of purpose and satisfaction. Many retirees find that volunteering keeps them active, socially engaged, and feeling needed, all of which contribute to long-term happiness.

13. Focus on Mental Health

Retirement can be a significant psychological adjustment. The loss of a structured work life may lead to feelings of aimlessness or depression. It's important to prioritize mental health by incorporating mindfulness practices, such as meditation or yoga, into your daily routine. Stay proactive in recognizing and addressing signs of stress, anxiety, or loneliness. Seeking professional counseling or joining a support group can also provide valuable tools for managing the emotional challenges that can come with retirement.

14. Pursue Passion Projects

Retirement is the perfect time to dive into projects that ignite your passion and bring you joy. Whether it's gardening, painting, writing, or woodworking, these activities give your life structure, challenge your creativity, and provide a sense of accomplishment. Passion projects can be deeply rewarding and are often the highlight of many retirees' daily lives. They offer a way to stay engaged, set goals, and continuously grow as an individual.

15. Stay Flexible with Your Retirement Goals

Life is unpredictable, and so are the circumstances that can arise during retirement. Stay flexible with your retirement goals and be willing to adjust as necessary. Financial markets may fluctuate, health may change, and family dynamics can shift. Being open to adjusting your plans ensures that you can adapt without feeling discouraged. Flexibility allows you to make the best of every situation while still pursuing your financial and personal goals.

16. Embrace Travel and Exploration

One of the joys of retirement is the freedom to explore the world at your own pace. Travel, whether international or local, offers new experiences, broadens perspectives, and provides memories that enrich your life. Plan trips to places you've always dreamed of visiting, or simply take the time to explore the beauty of your own region. Travel also keeps your mind and body active, introducing you to new cultures, foods, and ideas that stimulate your curiosity and sense of adventure.

17. Build a Balanced Routine

While retirement offers freedom, it's still important to have a routine that balances relaxation, productivity, and personal growth. Establishing a daily or weekly schedule helps ensure that you're making the most of your time while still allowing room for spontaneity. Incorporate time for hobbies, exercise, socializing, and relaxation to create a well-rounded lifestyle that keeps you engaged and content. A flexible but structured routine can prevent feelings of aimlessness and provide a sense of accomplishment.

18. Plan Your Estate Thoughtfully

Estate planning involves more than just distributing your assets; it's about ensuring your wishes are honored and minimizing potential conflicts for your loved ones. Create a comprehensive estate plan that includes a will, trusts, and healthcare directives. Regularly review and update your plan to reflect changes in your circumstances and legal requirements. Thoughtful estate planning provides peace of mind and ensures that your legacy is handled according to your wishes.

19. Prepare for End-of-Life Care

Preparing for end-of-life care involves making decisions about your medical treatment preferences and appointing someone to make healthcare decisions on your behalf. Creating advance directives and discussing your wishes with family ensures that your preferences are respected and reduces the burden on your loved ones. Planning for end-of-life care provides clarity and control during a challenging time, allowing you to focus on what matters most.

20. Celebrate Achievements and Milestones

Celebrating achievements and milestones in retirement reinforces a positive outlook and acknowledges your successes. Reflect on your accomplishments, both personal and professional, and celebrate them with family, friends, or through personal rituals. Recognizing and honoring these milestones boosts morale and provides a sense of closure and pride in your journey.

By implementing these 20 strategies, you lay the groundwork for a retirement that is financially secure, emotionally satisfying, and rich with opportunities. Each strategy contributes to building a balanced and rewarding retirement, allowing you to enjoy the fruits of your labor while living a life of purpose and joy.

CONCLUSION

Retirement is often seen as the culmination of a life's work, but in reality, it is a new beginning—a unique opportunity to redefine what fulfillment, happiness, and purpose mean for you. The transition from a career-driven existence to a phase where time, freedom, and choice take center stage is a profound shift. This journey is not just about financial security, but about designing a life that embraces the totality of your needs—financial, emotional, social, and personal.

Throughout this book, we've explored strategies that go beyond merely surviving in retirement to truly thriving. Whether it's building a solid financial foundation, safeguarding against market risks, or pursuing new avenues for learning and growth, each chapter offers tools to help you navigate this transformative period of life with clarity and confidence.

Key to a fulfilling retirement is the understanding that wealth isn't confined to numbers on a bank statement—it also includes the richness of your health, relationships, and sense of purpose. Retirement is a chance to reassess your priorities and make intentional choices that allow you to live with greater freedom and meaning. This holistic approach—balancing financial stability with personal growth, health, and social fulfillment—can help ensure that your retirement years are some of the most rewarding of your life.

It's important to remember that this phase of life is deeply personal. There is no one-size-fits-all solution, but rather, a range of possibilities that can be tailored to your individual goals and aspirations. Whether you're pursuing adventure through travel, finding joy in simpler living, or continuing to contribute to your community, retirement offers an opportunity to rediscover and reinvent yourself.

Embrace this time as a journey of self-discovery. Let go of any limiting beliefs about aging or fixed roles, and instead, step into this chapter with the confidence that you are still growing, learning, and evolving. With the right mindset and the strategies laid out in this book, you can craft a retirement that is not only financially secure but filled with joy, purpose, and connection.

Your golden years are a time to savor the freedom you've worked so hard to achieve. They are a chance to live intentionally and cultivate a life that is meaningful and true to your deepest values. Mastering retirement is about creating lasting wealth—not just in monetary terms, but in experiences, relationships, and personal fulfillment.

References

Financial Planning and Wealth Management

1. Bengen, W. P. (1994). *Determining Withdrawal Rates Using Historical Data.* Journal of Financial Planning, 7(1), 171-180.

2. Merton, R. C. (2003). *Thoughts on the Future: Theory and Practice in Investment Management.* Financial Analysts Journal, 59(1), 17-23.

3. Pfau, W. D. (2017). *How Much Can I Spend in Retirement? A Guide to Investment-Based Retirement Income Strategies.* Retirement Researcher Press.

4. Horan, S. M. (2009). *Private Wealth: Wealth Management in Practice.* CFA Institute Research Foundation.

5. Milevsky, M. A. (2012). *Are You a Stock or a Bond? Identify Your Own Human Capital for a Secure Financial Future.* FT Press.

Health and Wellness in Retirement

6. Rowe, J. W., & Kahn, R. L. (1997). *Successful Aging.* The Gerontologist, 37(4), 433-440.

7. McGonigal, K. (2015). *The Upside of Stress: Why Stress Is Good for You, and How to Get Good at It.* Avery.

8. Cress, M. E., & Meyer, M. (2018). *Physical Activity and Aging: A Handbook for Practitioners.* Human Kinetics.

9. Jeste, D. V., & Depp, C. A. (2010). *Positive Psychiatry: A Clinical Handbook for Caring for Older Adults.* American Psychiatric Publishing.

Psychological and Emotional Well-Being

10. Carstensen, L. L. (2011). *A Long Bright Future: Happiness, Health, and Financial Security in an Age of Increased Longevity.* PublicAffairs.

11. Lally, P. M., & Krystal, H. (2009). *Second Adulthood: The Guide to a Happy Retirement.* HarperCollins.

12. Lachman, M. E. (2006). *Development in Midlife.* Annual Review of Psychology, 57, 305-331.

13. Seligman, M. E. P. (2002). *Authentic Happiness: Using the New Positive Psychology to Realize Your Potential for Lasting Fulfillment.* Free Press.

Purpose and Meaning in Retirement

14. Ikigai, H., & Garcia, F. M. (2016). *Ikigai: The Japanese Secret to a Long and Happy Life.* Penguin Books.

15. Snowdon, D. (2001). *Aging with Grace: What the Nun Study Teaches Us About Leading Longer, Healthier, and More Meaningful Lives.* Bantam Books.

16. Van Prooijen, J. W., & Kuppens, T. (2013). *The Pro-Social Behavior of the Elderly: Age, Meaning, and Subjective Well-Being.* Journal of Happiness Studies, 14(2), 375-392.

17. Antonucci, T. C., & Akiyama, H. (1987). *Social Networks in Adult Life and a Preliminary Examination of the Convoy Model.* Journal of Gerontology, 42(5), 519-527.

Estate Planning and Legacy

18. Oshins, R. H., & Bove, A. L., Jr. (2006). *Modern Estate Planning Strategies: Planning for Retirement.* Trusts & Estates, 145(3), 62-69.

19. Langbein, J. H., & Stabile, S. J. (2006). *Pension and Employee Benefit Law.* Foundation Press.

20. Booth, A., & Brown, L. (2008). *The Family Legacy Handbook: How to Establish a Meaningful Legacy Through Philanthropy and Family Wealth Planning.* International Wealth Planners Association.

21. Helman, R., & VanDerhei, J. (2010). *The 2010 Retirement Confidence Survey: Confidence Stabilizes, but Preparations Continue to Erode.* EBRI Issue Brief, 340, 1-41.

About the Author

James A Smith, author of *Mastering Retirement: 20 Proven Strategies for Lasting Wealth, Happiness, and Fulfillment*, has dedicated his life to understanding and sharing the principles of financial independence and personal well-being. With over three decades of experience in finance and wealth management, is known for his practical, insightful guidance that has empowered countless individuals to achieve financial security and a fulfilling retirement.

Growing up in a modest household, Smith learned the value of financial discipline early on. His parents, hardworking and prudent, taught him to save diligently and live within his means. This foundation sparked a deep interest in the intricacies of wealth management and inspired him to pursue a degree in finance. After graduating with honors, he joined a prestigious financial advisory firm, where he quickly gained a reputation for his meticulous approach and client-focused advice.

Throughout his career, Smith worked with clients from diverse backgrounds, helping them plan for retirement, manage investments, and secure their financial futures. His role as a wealth advisor exposed him to the challenges many face when transitioning to retirement: uncertainty, identity shifts, and the pressing need for financial stability. Recognizing the importance of addressing these emotional aspects, Smith began incorporating holistic retirement strategies that encompass not only financial security but also personal fulfillment and mental well-being.

Driven by a desire to make retirement planning accessible to everyone, Smith embarked on a mission to write. His goal was to distill his years of experience and insight into a practical guide that anyone could use to build a prosperous and meaningful retirement. *Mastering Retirement* is the culmination of this journey—a roadmap to financial freedom, happiness, and purpose in one's later years.

Smith's approach to retirement planning emphasizes balance: achieving financial freedom while maintaining health, nurturing relationships, and finding a renewed sense of purpose. His work reflects a belief that a well-rounded retirement is possible through careful planning, strategic wealth management, and a positive mindset.

Beyond his career, Smith is passionate about lifelong learning and community service. He volunteers with local organizations that support financial literacy and serves as a mentor for aspiring finance professionals. In his personal life, he enjoys spending time with his family, hiking, and pursuing his love of travel, exploring new cultures and perspectives that enrich his own understanding of life and fulfillment.

Today, Smith continues to be a guiding voice in the world of retirement planning, inspiring readers to take charge of their future with confidence and clarity. Through *Mastering Retirement*, he shares the wisdom that has guided his own journey, offering a path for others to create a retirement filled with wealth, happiness, and purpose.

Disclaimer

The information provided in *Mastering Retirement: 20 Proven Strategies for Lasting Wealth, Happiness, and Fulfillment* is intended for general informational purposes only. The contents of this book do not constitute financial, legal, medical, or other professional advice. Readers are encouraged to consult with qualified professionals for advice specific to their individual circumstances before making any decisions based on the information contained in this book. Neither the author nor the publisher is responsible for any losses, damages, or liabilities that may arise from the use of this book or reliance on its contents.

Copyright

Copyright © 2024 by James A Smith.

All rights reserved. No part of this publication may be reproduced, distributed, or transmitted in any form or by any means, including photocopying, recording, or other electronic or mechanical methods, without the prior written permission of the author, except in the case of brief quotations embodied in critical reviews and certain other noncommercial uses permitted by copyright law. For permission requests, please contact the publisher.

Legal Notice

This book is a work of non-fiction and is intended to provide general information. Every effort has been made to ensure that the information in this book is accurate and complete as of the date of publication. However, the author and publisher make no representations or warranties, express or implied, about the completeness, accuracy, reliability, suitability, or availability with respect to the information, products, or services contained within this book.

All examples, stories, or references are used for illustrative purposes only. The author and publisher disclaim any liability in connection with the use or misuse of the information provided in this book. Any perceived slight of individuals or organizations is unintentional.

www.ingramcontent.com/pod-product-compliance
Lightning Source LLC
Chambersburg PA
CBHW071600220526
45469CB00003B/1074